CONRAD VOSS BARK

Fishing for Lake Trout

with Fly and Nymph

H. F. & G. WITHERBY LTD
4/5 PLANTAIN PLACE CROSBY ROW
LONDON SE1 1YN

Second impression, 1975

First published 1972

ISBN 0 85493 102 3

Printed in Great Britain
by Ebenezer Baylis and Son Limited
The Trinity Press, Worcester, and London

For

HOWARD MARSHALL

Acknowledgments

My thanks to Wilson Stephens, editor of *The Field*, Jack Thorndike, editor of *Trout and Salmon* and David Colquhoun, editor of *The Flyfishers' Journal*, for publishing articles of mine which contained some of the ideas which have been developed in this book; to Tim Rickett, secretary of The Flyfishers' Club, and George Tylor, the club librarian, for their help; and to Alex Behrendt, John Goddard, David Jacques, John Lawton, Ron Morgan, and Dermot Wilson for their advice, information, fly patterns and photographs.

I am grateful to many fishing companions over the years for much delight and unbounded amusement and instruction. They will forgive me, I know, if I do not name them but they have all in their various ways contributed something to these pages and I am in their debt; in particular my grateful thanks to Tom and Nan Kenny for their continual kindness and hospitality and to Howard Marshall for his invaluable encouragement and inspiration.

CONRAD VOSS BARK
April, 1972

Contents

List of Illustrations

I

Lake and Reservoir Fishing—A Dual Parentage—The Lure and the Fly

THERE is at the moment a considerable amount of confusion about fly fishing on lakes. Though there is a school of fishermen who are developing and practising fly fishing and especially nymph fishing on lakes and lochs and reservoirs they are still very much a minority. Many fishermen, especially if they have come to lake trout fishing during the last twenty or thirty years, believe that if they are using a fly rod then they are fly fishing. This idea is now so general that it must seem to be heresy to say that it is nonsense.

So let us begin with definitions.

If one is fly fishing for river trout one uses an artificial fly, a representation or suggestion of the natural insect, and this method of fishing follows a tradition which has been developed and refined by generations of fly fishermen for five hundred years at least, and possibly for much longer. Sometimes the fly is used floating on the surface, sometimes sunk below the surface, sometimes it is cast upstream and sometimes down. There are many ways of fishing the fly and in the last hundred years or so it has been discovered that when the fly is fished below the surface in a certain way it is probably taken by the trout as a nymph on its way to the surface to hatch; and from this discovery we have developed nymph fishing –

the use of an artificial pattern to represent the previous stage of the fly under water. Fly fishing on rivers, therefore, is fly fishing – the use of patterns suggesting either an adult or an immature fly.

On lakes and reservoirs the position is very different, very confusing and often bewildering. The vast majority of so-called lake flies do not represent flies at all and some are even deliberately designed to imitate snails and minnows. Because one can cast a cork-bodied imitation snail or a polythene-bodied imitation stickleback with a fly rod the idea persists that this is fly fishing.

To understand how this confusion arose we have to go back into history, to the development of salmon and sea trout flies, which are feathered lures, and were developed as such before the days of spinners. This is a separate development and a different kind of fishing. The confusion on lakes began, as C. F. Walker has pointed out, when reservoirs were opened and stocked with trout in England at the beginning of this century and the anglers who fished them – not knowing quite how to fish these huge stretches of water – used sea trout or salmon flies with some success. Later, trout fishermen using the traditional fly fishing method developed on rivers, discovered that this could also be applied to lakes. Two distinct types of fishing began, therefore, to develop side by side on the lake – salmon and sea trout lure fishing, acceptable enough as fly fishing in its proper context, and true fly fishing which had been developed for hundreds of years on rivers, and which was being adapted for lake fishing, either as dry fly or nymph.

Fishing for lake trout has therefore a dual parentage – a conflict between the lure and the fly – which has not yet been resolved and, rather surprisingly, frequently not understood. This has led to a great deal of confusion and bewilderment, if only in the proliferation of patterns of so-called lake flies and the choice that has to be made among the eight or nine hundred that now exist.

So, to begin with, one must be clear that there are two distinct types of fishing for lake trout – lure fishing and fly fishing – and of these lure fishing is a coarse and rough-and-ready method of fishing, involving little skill except in the matter of casting, and liable to cause a certain amount of damage to the fishing on some lakes, and especially on well-fished reservoirs.

On these reservoirs especially in the height of the season lure fishermen crowd together along the banks and stake out their claims to fish an area of water by sticking their landing nets point down in the mud and leaving them there. They wade out as far as possible and stand alongside their nets, often within ten or fifteen yards of their neighbours, and cast as far out as they possibly can. New methods of casting and the use of shooting heads enable them to cover a considerable distance.

Most of the insect life of lakes, however, tends to hatch in or near the margins. Deep and continual wading tends to destroy this life. The lack of marginal food and the continual disturbance of the water force the trout farther and farther out into the lake. It is a vicious circle. The longer the angler has to cast the less likely he is to see the take, the more he has to rely on the feel of the take, the faster he has to retrieve, and the heavier the tackle he has to use. Lure fishing – as I think Horsfall Turner once remarked – becomes a kind of feathered spinning. Continual long-distance casting and fast retrieves become wearisome if not boring.

Lure fishing is excellent and fascinating for salmon and sea trout. Indeed some of the happiest days of my life have been spent on the Spey. But the more I see of lure fishing on lakes the more convinced I become that it is a mistake and that in time either willingly or unwillingly we shall have to give it up in favour of the fly and the nymph.

Nymph fishing for lake trout is roughly more or less the equivalent of nymph fishing on rivers and streams, in that it is a delicate and difficult form of fishing which demands enormous concentration but which is exceptionally and extraordinarily rewarding in terms of excitement and intellectual stimulation. There is nothing quite like it, as any lure fisherman who has changed to the nymph will tell you, but it has one grave disadvantage. It is not easy to learn.

By comparison lure fishing is easy and for a lure fisherman to change over to nymph fishing is difficult because he will have to force himself to overcome many physical habits which have been engrained into his subconsciousness. Physical memory in fishing is very difficult to eradicate. It took me three or four seasons to do so and even now I sometimes find myself very tempted to use lure-fishing techniques – for example, to cast as far out into the lake as I possibly can just for the fun of it. In nymph fishing long casting is rarely necessary. Frequently it is a grave disadvantage. It lines the water. Any lure fisherman who changes over to nymph fishing is bound to catch fewer fish for several seasons until he acquires the new skills and forgets the old habits.

He will have to forget the impulse to wade out as deeply into the water as he can before he starts fishing.

He will have, in most circumstances, to forget about long-distance casting and in most cases will find it best to give up a shooting head for an ordinary double-tapered floating line.

He will not normally be able to fish in company, shoulder to shoulder, and he will rarely be able to fish the margins of reservoirs where deep wading continually takes place.

He will therefore have to walk to parts of the reservoir or lake which are not regularly fished, will have to learn how to read the water, how to fish the margins with a short line, how to take cover, and how not to disturb a feeding fish.

He will then have to learn how to make his nymph move like a nymph in the water, which will involve a great deal of concentration, and of imagination, and of delicacy in the touch of the fingers on the line. There is no automatic pull, pull, pull about nymph fishing. Every second the nymph is in the water there is intense concentration and intense mental activity, to ensure its correct movement and presentation.

The hands of a nymph fisherman on the lake must be as gentle and sensitive as a pianist's, capable of an infinite variety of touch.

It takes a period of apprenticeship. I fished a lure on lakes for fifteen or twenty years or more and when I changed to a nymph it was perhaps three years before I felt that I was really beginning to acquire the necessary skill. Even now there is so much to learn. It is an intensely physical pleasure – this delicacy of touch – but it is also an absorbing intellectual pleasure as well. The pleasure is in the skill. Sooner or later the pleasure of the skill will overcome you and from that moment on you will be lost with an absorbing passion.

That will be the start of the affair. From that moment you will never willingly fish a lure again. Maybe in some waters where the trout are after small fry you will be tempted to try a lure for a change but you will always come back to the nymph, with relief and gratitude.

Nymph fishermen have one advantage. They need never be troubled over the choice of fly. They can, if they wish, still carry many patterns. They can use detailed and exact imitations of the nymphs of the sedge, the pond olive, the claret dun, and so on, but there is no need for them to do so. One pattern of nymph in several sizes will be enough. A general pattern. A pattern that suggests a variety of underwater life.

Frank Sawyer has shown how one pattern of nymph – the pheasant tail – is sufficient for fishing the chalk streams. One pattern of nymph will serve for lakes also and I have found a palmer-dressed nymph in three or four sizes adequate for all the waters I have fished in England and Scotland. I see no reason at all why one pattern of nymph should not be enough for all lakes and reservoirs where there is a sufficiency of insect food to attract the trout. Once one has got rid of the anxiety as to whether or not one is using the right pattern one can then concentrate on the fishing, on presenting the nymph correctly, so that its movement deceives the trout into the belief that it is alive. It is – as Oliver Kite says – the movement that deceives the trout.

In the last seventy-odd years the development of fly fishing on lakes has made great progress. Although the majority of reservoir anglers are still lure fishermen they no longer use worms and spinners, as their fathers did.

When reservoirs were first opened for fishing towards the end of the 19th and the beginning of this century more or less any form of fishing was allowed.

In 1914, in one of the first books about reservoir fishing ever published, Ernest Phillips argued that worming and spinning were quite legitimate methods for reservoirs though he seemed to draw the line at maggots because of the natural distaste they might arouse among those who might hear of their use and might therefore imagine they would contaminate the water.

Phillips' book is important because he gives a list of some 152 reservoirs in the British Isles which were open for trout fishing by the year 1914. Of these, only 18 were reserved for fly fishing. Of the other 134 reservoirs most of them allowed fly and minnow fishing or else fly and worm fishing. Minnow fishing was allowed in parts of Blagdon and in Vyrnwy. At Ravensthorpe the boat fishing was fly only but minnow fishing was allowed from the bank. The Elan Valley reservoirs allowed the use of the fly, the worm, and the minnow; but for some reason or other at Thirlmere you could fish with anything except worm.

The attitude of Phillips – and one must suppose of most of the lake anglers of the time – was that, as he put it, the vital principle of angling was to catch fish by any method. 'It does not matter,' says Phillips happily, 'whether you offer a Zulu, a real mayfly, a worm, a minnow or a caddis grub.'

This is the legacy of the lake. It is a recent heritage. It still colours much of our thinking. The refinement of fly fishing on rivers took several hundred years. Lake fishing is still in its infancy. It is still using the coarse and indiscriminate methods of the Phillips era, except that the caddis grubs and minnows are now imitations and not real. That is the only change from the 1914 era.

It did not happen very easily. My maternal grandfather was a Bristol man by the name of Willie Cox and he fished Blagdon from about the time it was opened, in 1900 or so, until the middle 1920s. According to my father, Willie Cox was a hard-drinking man and a scenic artist of no little merit who used to work at the Bristol Theatre Royal, which in those days was known locally as the Old Gaff. But his passion was fishing and when they banned the minnow at Blagdon he said that he did not care a damn about that as he could produce an imitation minnow out of fur and feather which was just as deadly as the real thing and to hell with the Bristol

Waterworks. Old Grandpa Cox was as good as his word and he produced a minnow fly which was one of Blagdon's deadliest lures – or so my father said – and I have no doubt that this was so. I had one of Grandpa Cox's minnow flies myself until it was lost in the blitz of 1940 and it was a splendid looking creation, rather like a Dunkeld without the jungle cock. I tried some myself after the war and it caught some good trout.

Today they tie minnow flies with less fur and feather and more plastic, which makes them look more translucent, but they are still minnow flies, this illogical though workable compromise between two different styles of fishing. Lake fisherman still create artificial imitations of worms and snails and shrimps and sticklebacks. They still use salmon and sea trout flies to fish for rainbow and brown trout. Sooner or later, however, and I hope sooner rather than later, we shall progress from this stage, just as in most other human activities cruder and less cultivated tastes have given way to those which are more sophisticated and satisfying. So at least it has been for the rivers. It should happen also for the lake.

II

Grandpa Cox and the Blagdon Boil—Fly Spoons and Spinning Flies—A Twenty-Pounder?

My father used to tell me stories of Willie Cox when we went fishing together at places where Willie Cox had fished, mostly at Blagdon or on the River Chew or the Avon above Limpley Stoke, but Blagdon was his first love, and most of the great stories about Willie date from Blagdon in the days of Sheringham and Plunket Greene. Knowing about Willie as I do I find it annoying that some angling writers still believe that reservoir fishing methods of today were somehow developed only after the second world war.

I knew Grandpa Cox when he was very old – round about 1930 I suppose – and he was a gentle old man with a long drooping moustache and a vague manner. He leered at me a bit and winked an eye. He could fish and paint superbly well and was regarded by some of the family as an idler who neglected his wife and children because when he was not painting backdrops at the Old Gaff or drinking at the Llandoger Trow he would be off fishing at Blagdon and drinking at the Live and Let Live. But he could paint a lovely watercolour and I have one of his of Looe harbour which is a delight to see, so that even if my father was right in saying that Willie Cox was bone idle and semi-illiterate into the bargain, he had talent.

Long-distance casting methods of today would be a surprise to Willie only in the new materials and new techniques that are used – the shooting head and the monofilament backing and the rods of man-made fibre. Willie Cox and his generation used 14ft salmon rods, mostly made of spliced greenheart, to achieve distance, and according to my father Willie could put his fly from the edge of Green Lanes to Home Bay Point, right across the bay, and that must be a matter of 40 or 50 yards.

There would be very little new to Willie in the ideas of long-distance casting or of fishing deep. His big heavy silk lines were natural sinkers, certainly those that were used with his salmon rods. Alas, when he died the rods went to a friend and all I had were some of his flies and a few odds and ends, boxes and frog hooks. Did he use bait at Blagdon as well as minnow? I would not be surprised.

But Willie Cox's flies are important, perhaps more important now than I realized at the time. Rust and water got at them during the blitz in 1940 so that they more or less fell to pieces and became unrecognizable, but many of them I had used or had seen used before the war, and I have a good memory of most of the more interesting patterns.

There was the Blagdon green midge and the Blagdon buzzer and several small chironomids. These would date from somewhere around the 1920s – when Willie was experimenting with new methods, brooding no doubt upon the idea of exact imitation – and they were all mixed up in the box with huge heavy lures, some rather like the black lures of today but with much heavier hooks and weighted with lead wire, and – of course – his famous minnow flies and a number of traditional sea trout flies, such as the Peter Ross.

Some of his 'flies' were terrible concoctions that not

even the most dedicated lure fisherman of today would stomach, such as a large Alexandra with a small metal spinning vane just behind the eye of the hook which would revolve during the retrieve, and the fly-spoon – an ordinary fly with a small spoon attached to the eye which would wobble and flash in the water. There was also a kind of drone fly, made of some composition or other, with what looked like celluloid wings – a pretty exact imitation no doubt but as heavy as a stone, which would probably sound like a bumble bee in full flight when it was cast and would certainly sink straight to the bottom at a considerable speed.

To sum up the collection, it is clear enough that Willie Cox was deep-sunk lure fishing and long-distance casting seventy years ago, when Blagdon opened, and when – according to Phillips – the average weight of trout caught there was around 5 lbs, which has never happened in any lake before or since, if that figure is correct, and I have no means of knowing whether it is or not. All the evidence I have myself – or rather had because this too went in the blitz – was a photograph of some of Grandpa Cox's Blagdon trout. It must have been a day's catch and there was hardly a fish among the seven or eight of them under two pounds and three or four must have been five pounds or over.

It is also clear that Willie was not entirely satisfied with lure fishing. He would try anything which caught fish and towards the end of his life he was coming under the spell of Sheringham and Dr. Bell of Wrington, men who were advocating the use of the fly and of patterns which imitated the natural insects, the chironomid and sedge pupae and the nymphs of the pond and lake olives. Whether he was happy with the new methods I do not know.

Having got so far with Willie Cox I must tell the

story of the Blagdon 'boil' and the twenty pounder that once upon a time came up to Willie out of the depths.

My father told me the story as we were sitting on the banks of the River Chew at Bond's Bridge, near Chew Magna, a place that is full of magic for me because it was there I cast my first fly, but mostly we fished the worm, because the water was so thick. It is still thick today, drifting along like slow chocolate between high willows. Blagdon is half a dozen miles away and my father was telling me of the monstrous trout we would catch there when we could afford the guinea to go fishing.

There are times, my father said, now and again, very rarely, when the Blagdon trout go mad. On the evening when it happens, perhaps once a year, maybe once in five years, all the big trout from the deeps, the really big trout, are drawn to the shallows in one particular bay and there they fight and make the water boil with rises, and the sound of the water is so great that it can be heard for a mile.

One day, said my father, this happened when your grandfather was there. He was all alone. It was dusk. Suddenly the water began to boil. It was so big and strong and terrifying a sight that your grandfather's knees began to shake. He cast a fly at the boil and it was taken by a trout that was the biggest he had ever felt – and he had caught eight and nine pounders. But what he had hooked was far bigger than anything he had hooked before.

When that trout feels the hook, says my father, it dives for the middle of the lake and nothing stops it. The fish is so big and heavy it takes all the line and a hundred yards of backing, straight out, like a torpedo and when your grandfather realizes the fish is taking all his backing he tries to follow it and rushes into the lake, splashing water all round him in a great swirl of spray.

But he cannot run fast enough and he trips over and falls on his face. He manages to hold the rod above water but then there is a twang as the line runs up the end of the spool and snaps and the rod goes limp. The fish has taken his fly and his line and his backing as far off as Butcombe Point.

Your grandfather, says my father, was so distressed and shaken by his experience that he went up to the anglers' hut and drinks a bottle of whisky with his friends to console himself. But none of them believes him about the fish because he keeps on saying that it must have been a twenty pounder. There are no twenty pounders in Blagdon, says my father, and there never have been and never will be; but, he says, allowing for the fact that it was your grandfather it could have been ten.

And a ten pound trout, says my father, is no mean fish.

There is a sequel to the story of Grandpa Cox and the Blagdon boil which may explain some things about it and then on the other hand it may not. When I first heard the story about the boil I was a schoolboy and when I saw it happen or something like it happen myself it was thirty or more years later. Queer things do go on at Blagdon. Even Plunket Greene could tell you that there are times when the lake is bewitched.

I was fishing off Home Bay Point. It was in August and the evening was coming on, a slow heavy warm summer evening when the sticklebacks are in the shallows and the wind drops and the dusk comes down and the light fades. I was quite alone. There were no other anglers in sight. The lake seemed empty of fish. I was waiting for the evening rise and the surface of the water was as calm and still as a pool of pewter, dark pewter at that, because the light was going out of it and there were no reflections.

Near to nine o'clock the trout began to move, here and there, long heavy swirling rises, and suddenly I was in to a fish, a rainbow of about a pound and three-quarters, the first fish I had had that day. It took a long time to land and after that I began to play about with my flies and change to a thicker point and there was something wrong with the nylon and the knots came unstuck so by the time I was ready again it was nearly dark.

I had been hearing the plop and swirl of rising trout as I had changed my cast, now and again, here and there, but as I walked over the mud and stones towards the water the sound changed suddenly, within a matter of a few steps, and became continuous – the sound of churning water.

It was something I had not imagined possible and have never seen since – the continuous rise of many large fish within a very small and limited area. It is difficult to describe the size and extent of the rise with any accuracy but it was close inshore – in the shallows only a few yards out – and as I stood there the patch of disturbed water moved very slowly across in front of me from left to right until, after a few minutes, perhaps five at the most, it seemed to die out almost as quickly as it had started. The area of the disturbance was small, no more than a yard or so across and perhaps a yard or so wide, sometimes a little bit larger than that, but always focused at one central point which seemed to be in constant turmoil.

I had seen trout chasing sticklebacks many times before and I have seen it since but as I watched this thrashing and heaving patch of water it seemed to me to be something different. The difference was a matter of intensity and of the concentration of fish. The water was boiling with them. I remember now the trembling in my legs and the intensity of excitement there was in me as I cast my fly at this strange eruption.

On the third or fourth cast I had a take, a very violent take, and I knew that I was in to the largest trout I had ever hooked. It headed straight out into the lake and there was nothing whatever I could do to stop him. The fish ran and ran and ran and took out some seventy or eighty yards of backing – so much backing that there must have been only a few yards left on the reel by the time I was able to stop him. The fish was out very far and very deep and it stayed there, straining against the rod like a dog pulling at a leash – a most extraordinary experience, the kind of feeling you have when you are in to a big salmon which you cannot move.

There we were for some time – how long I have no idea but it seemed a lifetime – with the fish straining away from me and neither of us giving an inch. My legs were trembling violently and my wrist aching but somehow everything held, and slowly – oh, how very slowly! – the fish gave. The details of what happened next and how many runs he made I do not remember but I do remember I was eventually shaking too much to get him into the landing net which seemed to be far too small to hold him in any case, and I remember beaching him on the mud and falling on him and clasping him with both hands. It was a brown trout and when I weighed him later in the anglers' hut the scales put him at 4lb 12oz. The reason for his strange behaviour, the reason that he had felt like a salmon, the reason for that long straining pull out there in the depths was because he had been foul-hooked, in the pectoral fin, which was not really surprising when one considered how many fish must have been moving in such a small area. His stomach was crammed with sticklebacks.

This may have been the answer to Grandpa Cox's twenty-pounder. There was no doubt at all that this was the 'boil' – the Blagdon boil – of my father's story and with such a concentration of fish it is not impossible that Willie Cox had hooked an eight or nine pounder in one of its fins which had run out to the depths with such power that he had been broken. A foul-hooked fish feels twice as powerful and heavy as any ordinary fish. So that was possibly the explanation.

How can one be sure there are no twenty pounders in Blagdon?

Some people still think there are. Some years ago I was talking to a ghillie there who has now retired. I wish I could remember his name. He had known my father and my grandfather. I asked him what he was going to do when he retired and I found his answer so surprising that I can quote it from memory almost word for word.

'What I would like to do,' he said, 'is to get permission to mount a herring on a trace and troll it over there – and over there – where the water is deep, and see what happens.'

'Some years ago,' he went on, 'I caught a three pounder with scar marks across his back and belly. There's no pike in Blagdon. That fish had been taken broadways in the mouth of a bigger fish and had managed to escape. That I do know. I've seen those marks before on smaller fish but this was a big one – over three pounds it was – and those marks were fresh.'

He paused and lit his pipe.

'It would be a big fish that'd try to make a meal of a three pound trout, you know. Quite a big fish it would be. I have a theory that some of our big old brownies turn cannibal and live off our stock fish. Maybe it was one of those. A really big old cannibal. Well, anyway, what I would like to do would be to troll a herring around the deeps for a long long time – maybe spend weeks doing it – to see if we could find out.

He stopped for a little while and puffed at his pipe.

'I wouldn't be surprised,' he said, 'if there wasn't a twenty pounder out in those deeps somewhere. I know one thing – and that is you'll never get him on the fly.'

III

A Fly is a Fly—The Father of the Nymph—The Dry Fly on Lou Pesquie—The Self-powered Lure

To know something about fly fishing one has to know a little about flies. A sense of history is a good thing. It helps one to keep clear in one's mind that a fly rod was originally designed and is still intended for casting flies, not snails or fish, and that there is something unaesthetic and intellectually dishonest when one pretends that a plastic fish when cast with a fly rod is fly fishing. A fly is a fly.

Ever since the *Treatise on Angling* was published in 1496 the art or craft of fly fishing has been based on the principle of tying an imitation of the natural fly and casting it to fish that are rising to the natural insect. There are many variations of method and techniques. They are all based on that first great principle.

John Waller Hills was an M.P. at one time, but that was not a particularly important part of his life, and what was much more important to him was fishing, and in 1921 he published the best and most comprehensive history of fly fishing that we have. It illuminates and illustrates that principle far better than anyone else has done before or since.

Whether or not the English fly fisherman of the 15th

century fished upstream or down or wet or dry we do not know and it is not very important that we should know, but we do know that his aim was to cast his fly to rising fish. Possibly, in view of his materials, all that he could do was to fish with the wind behind him and let his fly dap about on the surface – rather like blowline fishing – but no one can be sure. But his flies were made of very similar materials to the flies we make today – the dun fly of 1496 is the same as our partridge and orange. By 1590 there were at least some fly fishermen who were attaching slivers of cork to their hooks to make their flies float. By 1651 came the first mention of reels and running lines. By 1724 silkworm gut was being used as well as the traditional horsehair casts. In 1851 came the first description of upstream dry fly.

And now we come to the nymph, which was not a word which meant quite the same thing to the fly fisherman of 1496 who thought that flies hatched from a miasma or from a brew and that nymphs were female spirits of the woods and glades. When the trout took their flies underwater, which I suspect they did more frequently than on the surface, I should imagine that they explained this by assuming that the trout was taking a drowned fly. It was not for several hundred years that the explanation came from the angler-entomologists that the sub-surface fly was more likely taken by the trout for a different insect altogether, the fly in its immature form of the nymph. In our own time we have the works of G. E. M. Skues and Frank Sawyer to explain nymph fishing methods on rivers. Much less is known about the first detailed account of nymph fishing on lakes. It was given in 1924 by a Scottish fisherman, R. C. Bridgett, in his book *Loch Fishing in Theory and Practice*, which was probably based on earlier articles he used to contribute to the Glasgow Herald.

So far as I can discover, Bridgett would seem to be the father of modern nymph fishing on lakes. He is at least a strong contestant for the title. Bridgett insists that 'it is the nymph which should receive the greatest attention' from the lake angler. He emphasizes the importance of midge pupa and of fishing midge patterns during a midge rise. He gives a first-class description of how to fish the deep-sunk nymph over weed beds from a boat, bringing it to the surface 'with a slow hesitant draw'. He dressed his own patterns – an olive nymph, a green nymph and a black nymph. They seem to be developments of the earlier olive, green and black spiders.

Bridgett uses the word 'nymph' to represent the nymphs of day flies as well as the pupae of sedges and midges – the pre-adult stage of surface flies. Entomologists may quibble over this but for practical purposes it seems to be a fair enough description for the angler. The important point to remember is that Bridgett was insisting on the importance of fly and nymph fishing on lakes at a time when most lake fishing was still lure fishing, either with the conventional Scottish loch flies or with some of the monsters in Willie Cox's fly box.

I must have fished lakes for years myself before it ever occurred to me that it was possible to fish them as we fish the rivers. This is part of the trouble. Lake fishermen are bedevilled by this inheritance of theirs, this conflict of styles, this legacy from the days of Grandpa Cox. Nor are they particularly helped by some of our contemporary journals which accept without question that lure fishing and fly fishing are somehow synonymous, and that the introduction of new and splendid fancy 'flies' every season is a right and proper part of progress. I have one advertisement cut from an angling paper which even now gives me a slight though delicious shudder to read. It is advertising flies. 'Fuzzy Wuzzy,' it says, 'is a right tickler and just the chap to get them going. Then there's Old Nic to put the wind up them and Sweeny Todd to polish them off. These trout flies of impeccable pedigree form the spearhead of a game fisherman's armoury. . . .'

The part that makes me shudder most is that delightful little bit about their impeccable pedigree forming a spearhead. Shades of Dame Juliana Berners and John Waller Hills! However, I suppose that I can put myself down as a purist of a kind and if that is so and if otherwise one has to use Fuzzy Wuzzies as right ticklers then I am glad of it. I would not be on their side.

But I must be honest. I have never used Old Nics and Sweeny Todds and I do not even know what they are, though they are certainly some kind of modern lure, but for many years I used lake lures of a similar kind, perhaps less luridly named, and it did not occur to me for many years that there was any better or more interesting method of taking fish. I look back on my ignorance with some astonishment but indeed why should I have known better? It took me years of experiment and much confusion and misunderstanding before I began to realize the distinction between a fly and a lure – that is to say so far as lakes are concerned – and I was not particularly helped by the angling writers of my generation, few of whom have made the distinction. Because of this for years it never occurred to me to fish a surface fly on a lake. I had been brought up on the assumption that lake trout do not take a surface fly, or that if they did they took it so rarely that it was not worth fishing it. I was under the fixed impression that dry-fly fishing on lakes was useless.

The truth is that dry-fly fishing on certain lakes and

at certain times is very deadly. I discovered this by accident, by treading on my box of line grease and getting my hands covered with it and getting so much grease on my fly that it was quite impossible for it to sink at all. It would have been just retribution if this accident had happened at Blagdon – where Sheringham had been so excited by dry-fly fishing – but in fact it happened to me on holiday when I was fishing a lake called Lou Pesquie in the south of France.

I had better tell the story of the dry fly on Lou Pesquie lake.

It is a small and delicate and beautiful pool in the pinewoods near St Auban, in the shadow of the Alps, and although it is three thousand feet above sea level it lies in a valley and the cliffs that hang above the lake are like the cliffs from Conan Doyle's lost world. You climb up to the lake along the Route Napoleon and turn off through a gateway of pines and follow a road that winds through the grassy fields like a grey snake. You plunge deeper into the woods and the mountains come up above you and then suddenly there is this glacier-blue lake and a car park and ice creams. The beauty of the lake is so great that in spite of the crowds it remains beautiful.

I had been searching for fishing because the sea was dirty and the coast roads were full of traffic – the south of France is no place to go in August – and so by chance I came to Lou Pesquie. There was no pollution but there were a great many Frenchmen fishing the lake with bubble floats and live grasshoppers. I explained to the *gardien* that I was a fly-fisherman and that I wished to fish the fly – the *mouche* I said, waving my hands, making up for my deficiency of French with an extravagance of gesture.

He seemed to understand. He became interested.

Very few people, he said, fished the *mouche* on his lake. It was not profitable. On the whole it was considered that one would catch more trout with the grasshopper. If my aim was to catch trout he would recommend the grasshopper, most certainly that was the bait, and if I wished to fish the grasshopper then I would be certain of a trout, of indeed many trout. On the other hand. . . .

Carefully he examined my flies. Perhaps that one, or that, or perhaps that. He was complimentary about my flies. They were beautiful. They were magnificent. There had once been a fly-fisherman there, many years ago, he could not remember, but he had done nothing at all, and the regular fishermen, being interested in catching fish, had sometimes caught flies and impaled them on the hook, but even with the real flies they did not do so well as with the grasshopper, but naturally I was a skilled fly-fisherman and assuredly I would catch many trout!

So I paid for my ticket and approached the lake. One side of it was wooded and the other side was a sloping beach. Along the beach the anglers sat in rows on little camp stools. Some had long bamboo poles. Others spinning rods. Mothers and daughters and girl friends sun-bathed in close proximity. Small boys – a veritable legion of small boys – hunted for grasshoppers in the long grass. There was a hum of insects and conversation and transistors.

I watched for some time and once or twice saw a bubble float bob and a trout hauled in and when that happened the successful angler would be besieged by small boys with their hands cooped round captured grasshoppers, offering their wares.

'I have a big one.'

'No, no, mine is much bigger and has just been caught.'

I did not feel somehow it was quite right for fly fishing. But, on the other hand, trout were rising out on the lake and they were not rising to grasshoppers. That – could that be? – a rise to midge? I searched my box for a midge or buzzer but the nearest thing I had was a hawthorn fly, a very small hawthorn fly it was true, but all the better for that, because a small hawthorn is not too unlike the duck fly – give and take the oddities of my way of dressing it – and if those really were midge hatching out there among the bubble floats I might have a chance.

I worked things out very carefully. A greased cast. Yes, it would need to be greased, and a fine point, a very fine point indeed, and perhaps the fly in the surface film, just breaking through. I was so embarrassed at being the odd man out – a *mouche* among the grasshoppers as it were – that I turned my back on the crowds to put up my rod. But I had been observed. Small boys surrounded me.

'No, no,' I said, in my best French, 'I do not use grasshoppers. See – here – I am using a fly.'

They stared and began to fade away from me, stepping carefully backwards from this madman. I laughed and waved my fly at them and dropped my grease tin and trod on it.

When I stepped to the bank it seemed to my fevered imagination that twelve dozen bubble float fishermen had stopped to watch. They had not, but that was how it felt. I was horribly exposed. Moreover there was a tree where my backcast ought to go and there were gentlemen on camp stools three yards on either side of me. My hands were covered in grease from trying to get the battered lid on my Mucilin tin and my rod was covered in grease and the cork handle was as slippery as an eel. When I wiped my brow that was greased too. Everything was greased.

The trout were still rising.

Somehow or other I managed to avoid the pinetree

and the first cast went out straight and true beyond the bubble floats to the centre of the rise. I did not see my fly fall but I saw the rise where it should have fallen and I was so surprised that I delayed the strike long enough to set the hook home as the trout went down. I made no more than six or seven casts and had four fish on the bank. Those hungry wild Alpine trout were going mad on a midge rise and one had only to leave an artificial floating there for a few seconds for it to be engulfed. I caught eleven trout in less than 40 minutes and then stopped because I did not want to catch any more. Certainly those trout would take grasshoppers. But what they lusted after was midge.

Suddenly there were men all around, shaking my hand, asking questions; men in berets with red and cheerful faces, brown-faced men wearing faded blue yachting caps, jostling to see the fly, to examine my box, to admire the rod, grasshopper men who had been beaten by the *mouche*. I remember the spattering outpouring of French, the long drawling vowels of Provence, my struggling explanations, my search for words, the impossibility of finding the French word for midge.

And the point of this story is not that there are times when the dry fly is a very deadly method of catching lake trout but simply that it is a most pleasant and delicate way of doing so and that if – like me – you are offended and revolted by the idea of impaling live grasshoppers on a hook you will be relieved and delighted that on that particular day at least two dozen bait fishermen and possibly more came to see that there was a more sophisticated and pleasant way of catching a trout than their own traditional method. Whether the grasshoppers around the shores of Lou Pesquie are now leading freer and happier lives I do not know but it may well be possible. I hope it is. Fly fishermen like to make converts. They are not evangelists in the Wesleyan sense of the word but they are not averse to a little salvation of the good things of life from time to time. If they can convert a bubble-floated Frenchman from impaling grasshoppers to the *mouche artificielle* then it is worth it.

It will be much more difficult to persuade the lure fisherman to take to the fly. There are already plastic grasshoppers in the shops over here – and plastic frogs as well for that matter – and I have no doubt that they will be as deadly as a Fuzzy Wuzzy or a Sweeney Todd when cast with a ten-foot reservoir rod out to the deeps. If it is legitimate fly fishing to cast plastic minnows I can see no logical reason why we should not receive a dispensation for plastic frogs. There may be worse to come.

According to a scientifically-minded angling friend of mine the next great invention in fly fishing will be the self-powered plastic minnow which in time may be produced reasonably cheaply. Inside the minnow will be a mini-motor, remotely powered and controlled. The minnow will not be cast. It will be launched.

The traditionalists will be sad to find their long rods and shooting heads and line rafts become obsolete but that is progress and the same thing has happened to gut and horsehair and split cane. The advantage will be great. They will simply launch their minnow from the side of the lake – fifty or a hundred yards away – where the trout are in hiding. Once it is in the fishing area it will cruise silently in circles, diving now and again, carrying out various minnowish manoeuvres, fishing continuously for as long as the angler pleases – or as long as the batteries last – until the trout takes. The trout can then be played and landed in the orthodox manner. According to our present conventions this, also, will be fly fishing.

IV

Ivens to Goddard – Lures and Imitations – A Confusion of Patterns

After about seventy-five years of the twin development of lure and fly fishing on lakes one would have thought that the confusion between the two would have been resolved. This has not been the case because apart from the work of a few writers like Bridgett – who is now largely forgotten – the distinction has never been made clear, nor have the reasons for making the distinction been apparent, and there have been no compulsions – theoretical or practical – which have forced lake fishermen to adopt one method in preference to the other. Lures, flashers, imitation bait, flies and nymphs – all are permissible and therefore in practice have become acceptable.

The modern generation of reservoir fishermen are to all intents and purposes unaware of any distinction between the lure and the fly; consequently the very delicate and more highly skilled techniques of nymph and fly fishing are confused with the traditional wet flies and modern lures and fished in more or less the same manner. But now the lure and wet fly men are using very specialized techniques and equipment which take them further and further away from the possibility of using the two methods side by side. This is why the time has come to make a clear distinction between two different methods of fishing. They are becoming more and more incompatible.

In 1953, T. C. Ivens published a book on reservoir fishing which has had an important and lasting influence. Ivens was well aware of the conflict between the lure and the fly and tried to resolve this as far as possible in a most practical way. He had discarded all the traditional loch patterns. In their place he simplified the choice of fly to eight simple representations – five of them being nymphs, and one a spider in the Phillips tradition, which could all be fished as deceivers – and the other three being lures which could be fished in circumstances when lure fishing was considered to be most necessary or effective. Among these lures was the now famous Jersey Herd, so called because the original body was tied with the copper foil from the top of a bottle of Jersey milk.

I have a great admiration for Ivens. He made an effort to resolve the problem. He established the importance of technique and codified much of the discoveries of the previous ten or twenty years. He tried very hard to establish his preference for nymph fishing over lure fishing, wherever this was possible, and the fact that he failed to do so can be blamed more on the phenomenal success of the Jersey Herd than on his original intention. The Jersey Herd became enormously popular. It still is very popular and is a most effective lure. It is so simple to fish. It is so easy. All that one has to do is to cast it a long way and then retrieve it fairly fast and the fish take.

By 1971, when the third edition of his book was published, Ivens had almost got to the stage where he felt at times rather regretful that he had designed the Jersey Herd. He had seen the way that lure fishing is abused, the trampling of marginal water, the crowding together, the long casting that drives the trout towards the centre of the lake. There is nothing that can be done, he feels, except to educate the fisherman in the way to behave. I am not so sure that he is right in this. So far as I can see, lure fishing contains within itself the dangers that Ivens fears. The exploitation of the methods of the lure lead inevitably to the behaviour which he would now seek to change. It is a simple method of fishing, rather crude, quite uncomplex, and without possibilities of development. Those who use this method will find little need to change from what are essentially bait-fishing habits – crowding and trampling through the water and staking out their swims.

The next important development in lake fishing came in 1960 with the publication of Commander C. F. Walker's book on lake flies. Walker was a great chalk stream fisherman who after he had given up fishing turned to what he called bug-hunting and produced a new series of fly patterns for lake fishing. They were based on close or perhaps exact imitation of some 28 of the most common underwater insects on which lake trout feed. He was, I think, the first to emphasize the great importance of the midge in lake trout fishing. I used Walker's patterns for several seasons. They have two great disadvantages. The first is that they are difficult to tie. The second is one of choice. When one has some 28 or more patterns in one's box and is faced with a large sheet of water without a trout in sight it is very difficult and sometimes I suspect almost impossible to know which of the 28 patterns one should begin to use. Walker was aware of the latter difficulty himself but it was not one he was able to resolve, at least for those anglers who lack his entomological knowledge.

Exactly ten years later, in 1970, came the third most important post-war book on lake fly fishing, also from an entomologist but also a great practical angler, John Goddard. In this book lake anglers have been able to see for the first time actual underwater photographs of many of the most common insects on which trout feed. For this alone it is invaluable. But the essential dilemma remained unresolved. Goddard tries to find a compromise between the fly and the lure by spreading the definition of the fly to include the imitation of snails and other forms of underwater life, but the dichotomy remains. Goddard's list of acceptable lake patterns includes 28 standard wet flies, 14 lures, 53 upwinged flies, 6 stoneflies, 26 sedges, and some 50 other patterns including beetles, shrimps and snails, a total of 177.

This is a brief and, I hope, not unfair summary of the three most important books on lake fishing to be published in the last thirty years. Ivens is a great technician and declares that the style of angling is of paramount and the fly only of secondary importance. Walker emphasized the importance of close or exact imitation. So, too, does Goddard, though as a very fine lake fisherman he accepts a compromise between the traditional loch patterns and the close or exact imitation of underwater insects of all kinds.

None of these writers has dealt with the main issue. For them it is quite a legitimate form of fly fishing to imitate a vast variety of snails, shrimps, and worms as well as small fish. Even C. F. Walker, who some would regard as a purist of the lake, produced patterns of shrimps and lice. He would not fish a water louse on the Itchen to catch a stock-reared rainbow. Why is it necessary to do so for the rainbows of the lake?

The answer, I believe, lies partly in the different appearance of a lake, partly in the different habits of lake trout – their habit of cruising in search of their food, for example – and perhaps mainly that the approach of the angler to the broad featureless acres of a reservoir should in some way be intrinsically different from his approach to a small stream. There is a certain amount of truth in all these arguments but in practice they lead inevitably to the same mistaken attitude to lake fishing that was made by our grandfathers in their approach to Blagdon. They widened and broadened their approach by using salmon and sea trout flies and the widening of the method of fishing led ultimately to the establishment of the simplest and least complicated of them as more or less standard practice. When, in our generation, the angler-entomologists began to turn away from this method they evolved the system of close or exact imitation of almost any kind of insect or fish – mainly I suspect from their own enthusiasm than from necessity – which did not in any way solve the problem but only made it even more complex than before.

At the latest count we now have some seven to eight hundred different patterns of lake 'flies' – most of them fancy lures, bucktails, streamers, and so on – mixed up with traditional loch patterns, plastic minnows, cork-bodied snails, and heaven knows what besides. For the newcomer to lake and reservoir fishing the confusion is almost entirely complete. It is certain to become worse. The number of effective lure and imitation bait patterns that can be created is possibly limitless.

I suffered from this proliferation of patterns myself for a number of years. When I got down to the water I was always faced with the problem of whether to fish a Greenwell or a Butcher or a Dunkeld. Eventually I found myself with something like four or five boxes crammed with six or seven hundred flies, but apart from the pleasure of fly-tying, which I always enjoy, the choice of fly became a torment. One could never be certain which was the right fly for the water. How was one to choose?

I then experimented, for a number of years, with 'flies' which are close or exact imitations of the natural insect, using Lane's and C. F. Walker's patterns. Here I came up against the difficulty, which Walker and Goddard freely admit exists, of choosing the insect on which it is assumed the trout may be feeding. It is true that both Walker and Goddard provide charts which show when the most common underwater insects are likely to be in season, but as I dislike taking books down to the lake, and as I am a poor entomologist, I found this of little help. I accept of course that the angling entomologist finds pleasure in the choice and selection of patterns but this is a minority and somewhat specialist field. The lure fisherman who wants to try to fish a fly is not likely to be encouraged to do so by having to make a choice among 56 upwinged duns and 28 sedges. He will return to the lure with relief at its simplicity.

The movement towards close or exact imitation of underwater insects is likely to be unproductive in other ways. It is possible to make lifelike copies of various creatures which will rarely if ever be taken by the trout for what they are because of the impossibility of imitating their movement. I suspect also that the difficulty of deciding when and at what season and at what place it is right to fish a corixa in preference to a shrimp is of mainly academic importance. Lake trout will normally 'take anything with the general form and behaviour of food'* and on those occasions when they are feeding selectively they are unlikely to be deceived by an artificial which cannot behave in the same way as the natural insect. Many of the underwater creatures in the Walker and Goddard lists loop or wriggle through

* T. C. Ivens, *Still Water Fly Fishing.*

the water in ways which no artificial can possibly imitate. Shrimp imitations are indeed taken by trout but whether as shrimps or merely something that gives the impression of being alive is impossible to say. I suspect that frequently it is the latter rather than the former.

Eventually I came to the conclusion that it was easier and simpler and less confusing deliberately to limit my fishing to fly fishing only and to see what happened. With fly fishing, of course, I included the nymph – the pre-adult form of water-bred flies – and thus brought myself into line with fly fishing on rivers. At first I was disappointed – and for those who may do likewise I am sure there will be many preliminary disappointments. When one has been fishing lures and fancy flies and copies of underwater insects it is not easy to concentrate on one method instead of several. The technique is not easy to acquire. During one season – at Weir Wood and Blagdon – I went for four or five days without a single fish. This was a time when by trial and error I was learning the methods which I will describe in later chapters of this book. They are not new methods. Ivens has described them and so has Goddard. So did Bridgett. But to read about them is merely a rough guide which has to be translated into action – and the technique is difficult.

The nymphs I use are suggestions – by no means imitations – of the nymphs of the pond olive and the lake olive. According to experts the nymphs of both these flies are found in most still waters of the British Isles. I have not yet discovered any disadvantage in restricting myself to the use of these nymphs. Two of my largest trout – one of nearly five pounds and the other of over eight pounds – have been taken on them – and the five pounder took my nymph while chasing sticklebacks and the eight pounder who took it had its stomach full of snail. I have not discovered any difficulty in persuading trout that have apparently been feeding selectively on other insects to take a well-presented nymph. Indeed I have discovered no disadvantage at all in restricting myself to the nymph. On the contrary, the advantages have been far greater than I realized when I decided to make the change. I had no idea of the pleasure that was in store.

I do not think it was really until the third season of my experiments that I began to fish the nymph successfully. This is understandable. One has to concentrate on many aspects of fishing that previously could be ignored. It was, I think, almost second nature for me to arrive at a lake or reservoir, put up a fly, and then wade out some distance from the shore to make my first cast. A nymph fisherman will, preferably, never wade at all for his first cast. It was at one time almost second nature for me to cast out as far as possible into the lake. In contrast, a nymph fisherman will cast as short a line as he possibly can. A lure fisherman will not mind if the water he is fishing is disturbed by pick-ups and splashy casting. In nymph fishing this is fatal and must be avoided at all costs. This is what I mean by saying that the two methods are incompatible and no lure fisherman can change to a nymph without a long period of readjustment and retraining. It needs consistent and concentrated effort. The nymph fisherman also needs to fish alone. He must avoid any disturbance to the water. He must get away from the crowd. Even on well-fished and overcrowded reservoirs this can be done. But it is not easy. Nothing about nymph fishing is easy. That is why it is so rewarding.

It was, as I say, my third season with the nymph which was so successful. This was when I was able to adapt the system of the 'induced take' from river nymph fishing to the lake. The induced take – so ably described by the late Oliver Kite in his book on fishing the nymph on chalk streams – is a method by which the nymph is suddenly accelerated upwards as it approaches the fish. In the chalk streams, of course, one can often give a sudden acceleration to the nymph as it approaches the trout, because one can see the fish and estimate the path that the nymph is taking. In lakes this is often not possible and most induced takes must be given blind, as it were, in the hope that a cruising trout will suddenly see it. The speculative nature of an induced take in lake fishing is of course lessened if one can cast to a rising fish, or a fish one can see cruising; even so it is a slightly different technique to that used on rivers though basically the principle is the same – the sudden acceleration of the nymph which causes an almost automatic response from the trout.

Nymph fishing is very different from fishing the wet fly or the lure. It requires considerably more skill. The question that I suppose one must ask, if one is fishing a lure, is whether there is an advantage in making the change.

V

The Constant Nymph–Selective Feeding –Practical Methods

THERE are several very good reasons why one should return to true fly fishing for lake trout and give up fishing loch flies – sea trout flies – and lures. There is the matter of the more interesting character of fly fishing, a more absorbing variety of techniques, an escape from the occasional tedium of long-distance casting, and a relief from the perpetual dilemma of the choice of fly.

The objections that lure fishermen will make include the old argument that lake trout are accustomed to eating small fry and therefore will disregard a nymph, that in any case they prefer long-distance casting and fishing shoulder to shoulder in company, and that they do not mind any legitimate method of fishing so long as it catches fish.

On the first point, this is simply not true – my own records and those of other nymph fishermen show that lake trout will take a nymph even when chasing stickleback shoals providing the presentation is correct. That proviso of course is all-important. Presentation does require more skill and delicacy than that of the lure. It has to be learnt. But the other points can, I think, be disregarded. They are a matter of taste. For those who are, for whatever reason, dissatisfied with the lure, nymph fishing does open the possibility of an escape to a more satisfying and absorbing method. In one sense, the method is simple – that is to say simple in principle.

It was Howard Marshall who once wrote that he would not have fishing overlaid with science. In the same way, I would not have it overlaid with complexity. The angler-entomologists have become too intricate and devious in their passion for creating exact copies of lake flies. Who but an entomologist is going to choose among the *56* patterns of up-winged duns given in Goddard's list if he can fish but one? On all occasions I would lean towards simplicity. It relieves my worry about changing flies, wondering whether I should go from a pond olive to a claret dun, or possibly a sepia dun. I salute those who take this trouble but it is not for me. I find that to use only one pattern of fly is a wonderful way of concentrating the mind on the matter of its proper presentation to the fish. A man who worries too much about his flies wastes time and effort which could well be concentrated on more important business.

And do not forget that to make a choice of fly is really a serious and anxious business if you are carrying two or three boxes of them in your pockets as you walk down to the lake. I remember I worried myself for years wondering whether this was a black and peacock spider day, or perhaps one for the Wickham, or perhaps the weather was ripe for a Dunkeld. I would end up with choosing a Peter Ross, fish for an hour or so, and then a nagging thought would occur that perhaps after all this was not the time of year for the Ross. Off it would come and on would go another fly, and then a little later another, and then another, until I ended in a fine state of mental confusion – or a fish – whichever happened to come first.

The nymph is constant.

If one makes the effort to master the presentation, confusion is at an end.

These are some of the advantages. But there is, I think – and in fishing one has to speak personally, according to experience – several far greater advantages which are somewhat difficult to capture and define. There is something which one can only describe as an aesthetic satisfaction which I never experienced with the lure, however delicately and gently it was fished. One pulls it in at a reasonable pace, perhaps varying it from time to time, and when the trout takes it does so in most cases with a bang. One feels the fish. One does not need to concentrate very much on watching the line. The next time you see lure fishermen in action, watch how they will look away while they are fishing, talking to their neighbours, pulling in the line all the time yet often glancing away when something catches their interest. Perhaps it is very bad fishing but this is often what happens.

In contrast, while fishing a nymph, only very rarely will there be a bang on the line to indicate a take. A take is indicated nine times out of ten by a slight movement of the line. Therefore, in order not to miss a take, the nymph fisherman is concentrating all the time, never taking his eyes off the end of the line or the floating nylon beyond. He will strike on the slightest movement. The concentration – and therefore the absorption and excitement – are intense. This, again, is only one factor. Another is the development of watercraft – the search for fish, the concentration that is necessary to imitate the movement of the nymph, the delicacy that is needed in casting. All these add up to a total intellectual and physical absorption and concentration on the task in hand. Concentration can go quickly and then one needs to rest, but in resting there is always for me a sense of

Plate II

Early Reservoir Flies

Lures and artificial baits which were in use during the early years of reservoir fishing, approximately from 1900 to 1925.

The dilemma of those years is clearly shown. Spinning baits were dressed up as flies. At the same time efforts were being made to create exact copies of a whole range of natural insects.

Top row: A black beetle with celluloid wings, a maggot or caddis of wool and silk, and a red spider or midge.

Second row: Alexandra lures with treble hooks, one with an extra treble in front of the spinning vane.

Third row: A traditional mallard and claret dressed on a salmon hook, and a black beetle about one inch long.

Fourth row: A golden beetle, a ladybird about three times life size, and a hornet with celluloid wings.

Bottom row: Two minnow "flies" – the one without spinning vanes designed to comply with fly-only restrictions. They weigh over half an ounce, the hard bodies are closely bound with silver tinsel, and the back and tails are of brown mallard.

These lures and "flies" are similar to those used by Willie Cox on Blagdon but the collection from which this photograph was taken was discovered by Terry Howe in a secondhand shop in south-east London.

Modern Reservoir Lures

The "minnow fly" of the early part of this century was much less sophisticated than these two popular modern lures, the Polystickle (top left), a dressing by Richard Walker, made from plastic materials, and (top right) the Jersey Herd, so-called because the original dressing by T. C. Ivens used copper-coloured foil for the body, cut from the cap of a bottle of Jersey milk. Both are excellent imitations of small fry.

The six patterns below include traditional wet-flies, mainly though not entirely of Scottish origin, which are now widely used in lakes and reservoirs as well as for sea trout. They are the Butcher; Teal, Blue and Silver; Black Zulu; Alexandra; Peter Ross; and an Invicta. Without the wing, and with mixed palmer hackles, the Invicta is a not dissimilar fly to one of Kingsmill Moore's Bumbles. Most of these patterns are an inch or more in length, dressed on 6 and 8 hooks. The Polystickle is nearly an inch and a half from eye to tail.

exhilaration even if there has not been a take. I am always thinking what to do next and how to do it.

I suppose one could summarize the argument by saying that in nymph fishing one has to exercise far more skills than in the more primitive or more coarser forms of fishing and that the intellectual and physical satisfaction in practising these varied skills is so great that once having experienced them to the full it is almost impossible to go back. This is why – in my experience – a lure fisherman who takes the trouble to acquire the ability to fish the nymph successfully will never return to the lure without a sense that something is missing, that he is no longer exercising his talents to the full.

A great American fly fisherman, George La Branche, once wrote that just as one gets greater satisfaction and pleasure from good music when one graduates to it from the poorer sort, so too does the angler who graduates to the higher forms of fishing from cruder and coarser methods. It sounds like the argument of the purist but one cannot dismiss it by a word, or smear it in a phrase, especially when one recognizes from one's own experience that there is a great deal of truth in what he says. The sad business is that so many young fishermen, taking up lake fly fishing for the first time, and being educated in the lure, may pass most of their lives in ignorance of all else. They will miss the intense pleasure of true fly fishing.

However, I would not wish to put only one side. The greatest challenge to the theory of nymph fishing comes from the problem of selective feeding. According to Ivens, lake trout are not selective feeders. This may possibly be confirmed by the analysis of stomach content. But Goddard and other writers provide evidence that lake trout do feed selectively on one type of food.

It depends, as Joad used to say, on what one means by

selective feeding. I remember casting to and catching a beautiful rainbow in the Border Pool at Two Lakes which had been gulping down huge quantities of small black midge, very small black midge, the kind you would try to imitate on a number 18 hook. He took my golden-olive palmer-dressed nymph on a number 12 hook without hesitation when I had presented it to him correctly, that is after a dozen or more failures. His stomach and gullet were crammed full of midge. Had he suddenly changed from being a selective feeder when he saw this somewhat larger offering even though it was of a different size and shape and colour? Did he take it by accident, or had he seen it several times and decided there must be some of these nymphs about again and that it was time for a change? Or did he take it in fury and anger at some other creature which might even be feeding on the midge itself? I do not know.

The answer must lie within one's own experience. If trout where I have been fishing have been feeding selectively on certain insects and refusing others then I must have shared in a common experience. On the other hand where I have assumed, mainly by their stomach contents, that the trout have been selectively feeding, and when they have taken my nymph, I have not been aware that I have been less successful than others who have been attempting to catch them with imitations of the natural insect. My results with the nymph have been reasonably constant and over the three seasons that my pattern has been in use I have become much less concerned about the matter of selectivity and much more concerned about my own method of presentation. It is the way the nymph is put to the trout that matters most.

There is another theory about selective-feeding trout which has been put to me and which must be considered. There is no certainty about these things. They are delightful subjects for speculation. This particular theory is that my nymphs are palmer dressed, deliberately so, so that the buzz of small hackles which go down the thorax and for most of the way down the abdomen give a certain effect of translucency and of movement, which is in fact what they are intended to do. The suggestion is that in certain waters and under certain conditions of light this palmer dressing creates mainly an effect of translucent light surrounding an opaque body – what Skues called the 'sheer sparkle' of hackles – and that in these circumstances what I call a nymph may well be taken by the trout for another insect. The hackles may give the impression of an inner movement, a wriggle effect if you like, which might correspond to the looping of a midge pupa. The trout, it is suggested, may take my nymph for a midge.

I must say I rather like this theory though I have not the least idea whether or not it is correct. But if my dressing does suggest to the trout that my nymph is also another insect, from time to time, when this is appropriate, I would not like to destroy the illusion. Good fly dressing is the creation of illusions.

It is an open question – one of those delightful mysteries about which speculation can be endless. All that seems to matter in practice is that I have not yet found an occasion when I have been aware of being handicapped by using a nymph and that if the number of fish caught over a season is the criteria of judgment – and certainly this is a major though not the only factor – then during the last season with the nymph my total catch was up by some twenty per cent. This again is no proof, nor do I submit it as such, but it can be taken as an indication of a trend. If selective feeding was widespread then one would have expected the indications to go the other way.

It is not generally realized, of course, what an enormous mass of insect life is readily available for eating, and what an infinite variety there is at hand. Alex Behrendt who runs the Two Lakes fishery at Romsey, in Hampshire, once took out some 80,000 small tench from three of the lakes. He wrote to me about this as follows:

> We carefully worked out the average and found that fifteen tench weighed one pound. According to my figures that makes 5,333 pounds weight of tench and as these fish are purely eaters of small water creatures – they are not vegetable eaters – and if one accepts the figures of all the experts that seven pounds of food produces one pound of fish then these tench must have eaten 37,331 pounds of food. Can you imagine the number of shrimps, nymphs and snails needed to make up this amount? It is unbelievable! And Two Lakes is not an exception. Other well-managed lake fisheries produce the same food.

And when one considers that the average weight of trout caught at Two Lakes is 2·4 pounds – or thereabouts – and some 6,000 trout are caught every season we come up against astronomical figures. There are clearly hundreds of tons of insect life available at these small two- and three-acre lakes, while at places such as Grafham and Chew there must be thousands of tons. All of which points to the conclusion that with such a rich variety of food available selective feeding may not be such a great problem for the lake fisherman as some may imagine. One can argue about these things for a long time – for example, to what extent do trout eat daphnia and other forms of tiny life. Are they souping up plankton from the surface when all that the angler sees is a hatch of midge and finds that the trout will not take his copy of the artificial? This is all splendidly provocative stuff but it is best to leave it to the entomologists lest we get in waters that are too deep for us.

So let us go on to practical methods of fishing the nymph.

They are, on the whole, marginal creatures, living in the mud and weed beds on the edges rather than in the depths of lakes. Before they rise to the surface to hatch into the dun they can be fairly active when disturbed, and move quickly, but when rising to hatch they are inclined to rise slowly to the surface, sometimes resting, sometimes sinking a little, until they come to the surface film. The transformation into the dun is then said to take place fairly quickly after a certain amount of twisting and turning while the insect pulls itself from the shuck or outer skin. The gill plates along the sides are a noticeable feature of the lake and pond olive nymphs but to what extent they are always active during the ascent I do not know. Nevertheless I always tie my nymphs buzz – the palmer dressing – in the assumption that the buzz of fibres suggest the movements of gills.

Nymphs can be fished quite deep near weed beds or in mid-water or just below the surface. We will deal later with deep fishing. In practice mid-water and sub-surface fishing tend to merge into one another so that the main characteristic of what I call sub-surface fishing – which does include mid-water – is the fact that this is using a greased cast and a reasonably small nymph. The usual size of nymph for sub-surface fishing is about a number 12, Redditch scale, slightly weighted with lead or copper wire in the region of the thorax – that is behind the eye of the hook but not too close to the eye because this would interfere with the tying of the hackle.

The rod should be medium actioned and the length is not particularly important. I use a split cane of about 8ft 6in, but would be quite happy with a reservoir rod of 9 ft or more. I use a double-tapered floating line with a loop whipped on the end. I mention the loop because when fishing the nymph it is of enormous importance not to create line wake in calm water conditions. It may be my fancy – one does develop fancies of this kind – but a loop seems to create less of a line wake than a knot.

The length of the nylon cast or leader is of very great importance indeed. It should be about 12 ft long. For Blagdon or Two Lakes I loop about 6 ft of 15 lb breaking strain nylon on to my line and to this I attach a point about 6 ft long of about 5 lb (2x) breaking strain. For Weir Wood one can drop to a point of about 4 lb (3x) and for a Scottish lochan 1½ lb (6x). One can also buy beautifully tapered nylon casts without any knots in them at all and though these are somewhat expensive they are delightful to use. But they are generally no more than 9 ft in length so that again one needs a heavy yard of nylon between the top of the cast and the line to give the necessary length. The long leader is used to avoid lining the fish. The shadow and splash of a line on the water are sure ways of scaring off trout and certainly of stopping them feeding. Leaders longer than 12 ft would be useful but are difficult to control and cast, though Goddard has used leaders of up to 16 ft.

For sub-surface nymph fishing the nylon should be greased sufficiently to float. It is a matter of judgment and experience how much of the nylon to grease. Certainly one should grease the heavy nylon part – the 6 ft length between the line and the point. Very often when I start fishing I will grease the whole of the nylon down to a foot or so of the nymph. After some hour or so of fishing the weight of the nymph may gradually sink the whole of the point even if it retains some of the grease. For deep nymph fishing of course the whole 12 ft of nylon remains ungreased. For sub-surface fishing the heavy part of the nylon should always be greased. These are rough guide lines to follow rather than hard and fast rules.

Let us assume we are going to fish Two Lakes which, with Blagdon, shares my deepest affection. Do not let us make it too easy. Let us imagine it is one of those bright sunny days in mid-summer, a very calm day with hardly a breath of wind on the water, the sort of day when things are likely to be dour.

Off the Romsey road and down through the pinewoods we go to the car park, which is a clearing in the trees, and in front of us is Alex Behrendt's house surrounded by a lawn, and as we park the car out from the house come bounding his two Alsatian guard dogs, barking vigorously. They are there to keep off poachers, and very necessary it is too, so therefore it is also necessary to behave as though one is not a poacher to avoid being bitten. I am never quite sure how this is done and on one occasion when I was obviously behaving badly one of them nipped my fishing coat. This morning, however, we seem to be accepted for what we are, and the dogs, having done their duty as guards, return to the house. We put up our rods, our long leaders, and our nymphs, grease the casts, and all is ready. We walk through a little screen of trees and on our left is the Home Pool, shining in the sun.

VI

Fishing the Nymph – Sub-surface – The Induced Take

Do not approach the water like a lure fisherman. That is the first thing to learn. In most lakes and reservoirs the marginal feed is frequently the richest. Trout will feed close in to the shore, often in shallow water, providing they are not disturbed. Alex Behrendt will tell you the story of how he looks out of his bedroom window, from which height he can see clearly down into part of Home Pool. Three or four trout will be lying close in to the bank – maybe a yard or so out – and an angler will walk past them, on the way to one of the other lakes, so he is not close to the edge, perhaps two or three yards away. Even so, the trout sink down out of sight. A little while after the angler has passed and all is quiet and there is no movement and no vibration the trout will slowly rise to their former positions. Now they may feed again. They will never feed while they are disturbed.

Home Pool is an ideal place to fish the nymph because there is good cover. At the edge, near the house, there are small bushes here and there and between these bushes the grass edges are well trampled. Do not stand in one of these gaps. Stand close to a bush, behind it if possible, so that you have cover. Move quietly and slowly. There are no visible rises but remember you are stalking fish and even though you may not see a trout the likelihood is that he is there. You must work on that assumption.

To begin with you are not going to fish the water directly in front of you at all. You are too close to it and if there are fish there they may already have noticed a movement behind the bush. You must assume that the few yards immediately in front of you are dead water.

You will start by searching the water on either side of you. Assume that the bank is the base line and straight out in front of you is 90 degrees. You will begin fishing with short casts at an angle of some 20 degrees or so to your left, increasing this to 30 or 40 degrees, and when you have searched the water to your left you can begin the same search to your right, again starting close in to the bank.

Your first cast at 20 degrees to your left will be very short with as little of the line as possible on the water, and then the next cast at 30 degrees will still be very short, and so on at 40 degrees. Then come back to the 20 degree position and lengthen your line a little. This is a way of searching the water without scaring the fish. Naturally you will not take all this business about 20 or 30 degrees exactly; it is merely a convenient method of explaining the technique. You can make many variations on this as long as you understand that the idea is not to line the fish – to put your heavy line over fish that are feeding or else are ready to feed. Your nymph should always be searching water that has not been lined and not been fished before. The ideal is to try and put the nymph in front of a trout without showing him even the point of the nylon, never mind the heavy nylon or the line. Only when you have searched the water thoroughly on both sides should you cross the dead water in front and lengthen your line to fish straight out ahead of you, starting as short as possible, lengthening gradually.

Let us begin with the first cast to the side – to your left where the weeds come close to the bank. It is fairly shallow there but big trout sometimes lie under those weeds, feeling secure under cover. Keep a short line – not much more than the length of your rod to begin with – and remember that you have to straighten out 12 ft of nylon at the end of it. You will get your nymph out quite far even though it will be nothing like the distance you have been used to with a lure. You feel it is hopeless with such a short cast? I know the feeling. I told you before that there are many subconscious feelings, many aspects of physical memory, that will have to change. The best thing to hope for is to catch one or two trout fairly quickly close in because there is nothing like proof that it can be done to convince you. Alas it may not happen.

Cast a short line to your left. Watch your fly as it falls near the weeds, no more than a yard or so out from the bank and little more than seven or eight yards away from you. Keep under cover. If there is a trout there and he sees only the nymph he may take. If he sees the nylon point he may or may not take. But if he sees your movement behind the bush he will freeze. This is delicate work.

What is wrong? The fly shows no inclination to sink. Although it is a weighted nymph it is still floating on its palmered hackles. No – don't touch it, don't disturb the water, let it rest there on the surface for a moment. This is not because I want you to fish 'dry' – nothing of the kind. The point is that when you approached the water you may have made a slight sound or moved too quickly and you may in this way have disturbed the fish. They may still be 'frozen' – having sunk down towards the bottom. When you cast it might have been an additional disturbance. If you twitch the line now to make the nymph sink in these calm conditions you will create another disturbance. Instead – let everything go quiet for a little or, as some would say, give them a chance to look at the fly.

There may not be a fish there, of course, but you must assume there may be, and you must remember never to make an unnecessary noise or an unnecessary movement. Let the fly bide. It will sink – in time – though if you do become impatient you can try a very very slow retrieve, a slow gentle pull of a few inches every five or ten seconds. Yes – as slow as that. You are fishing a nymph, not a scuttering sedge.

Now the nymph is sinking through the film. The dubbing has become waterlogged. The nymph goes under and the nylon follows. Bring the nymph in gently. You must have a feeling that you are stroking the water. You will see the point where the nylon enters the water. The nymph is somewhere below. When you pull the line you will see, on the calm surface, a slight wake forming behind the nylon as it is pulled through the water. If you are seeing line wake, you are retrieving too fast.

In calm water conditions line wake must never be visible. Or shall we say that your chances of taking a trout are likely to decrease if surface ripples draw its attention to the glint of the nylon. Your whole aim and object is to present the nymph to the trout as though you and the rod and the line and the nylon cast were non-existent. So, gently and steadily draw the nymph towards you. Glide it along, very very slowly.

If you are holding the rod in your right hand then let the line go through the fingers of the right hand and pull the line gently and steadily with the left. You may pull six or seven inches at a time, if you wish, but let this motion take about five seconds, pause a little, and then repeat. This simple smooth gliding movement is not easy. It takes practice before you get the nymph travelling slowly and smoothly through the water without disturbance. When you have mastered the simple gliding pull then you can experiment with other movements – a slow gentle pull and then a long pause to allow the nymph to sink down, then a slight twitch but not strong enough to cause line wake, then a very slow lift that begins to accelerate as the nymph rises to the surface. The permutations of movements seem to be as many as any man can invent.

Now – this is very important. Bring the fly in to the side as close as possible – within a yard or so of your feet if you can. Never furrow the surface of the lake, even close in, by dragging line off the water. Bring it gently to the side and when the fly comes to the surface lift off gently and cast again, using as few false casts as possible. You are beginning to understand what is meant by the words used in *The Compleat Angler* and used every generation since – 'Study to be quiet'.

Remember these are calm water conditions. Many loch fishermen will tell you trout cannot be caught in a calm. It needs, they say, a ripple on the water. The ripple masks line wake and splash and the noise of heavy casting. Remember that sound is magnified under water. If you have ever swum under water you will know what I mean. Sound – the vibration of sound – is a deadly enemy to all fishermen. The trout freeze. They stop eating. So you must cast as lightly as a feather, keeping as little line on the water as you can, drawing off line without drag or furrowing the surface. You must learn to develop what the artist or musician would call sensitive hands, powerful but with an exquisite delicacy of touch.

Never disturb the water.

Begin to think like a nymph that is rising to the surface to hatch into a fly. By this I mean you must imagine what your nymph is doing and manoeuvre it so as to give it the resemblance of life. This needs a great deal of concentration.

Imagine the little creature rising towards the light, sometimes sinking again, resting, rising again perhaps a little more quickly, then gliding along under the surface, trying to break through the surface film. Fix this image in your mind and then try to convey these movements down the line and along the leader towards the fly on the point. Use only one fly, by the way. Avoid anything which will create any complication, any additional splash. A dropper is for wet-fly fishing, not for the nymph. Use your nymph delicately. Follow the image of its movement in your mind. Try to convey this through the touch of your hands. In time, this will give you intense pleasure – this working of the fly. If you play chess you will know what I mean when I speak of the intense pleasure of concentration.

Well, now, make a second cast and this time put the nymph a little farther from the bank – but still casting to your side along the line of the shore. Keep your line short. If you are well hidden, have made no noise, and there are trout there, they may well take. They may not. Who can say? But there are no fish showing so you must search the water for them.

Still keeping to the side cast, strip another yard of line off the reel so that next time your fly will fall that distance farther on. Then, the next time, alter the direction of your cast, and search that new area of water. You can alter the pattern as you will but always you are fanning out the fly, searching new areas of water, extending the cast yard by yard. Now, still casting along the shore at an angle of twenty or thirty degrees, you may have ten or fifteen yards of line out and the fly may be fishing eight or ten yards from the bank.

Leave that side for the time being and begin to search the water on your other side. Only when you have explored both sides thoroughly should you try a cast out in front of you. Keep that short to begin with, gradually lengthening, yard by yard, until – if you are so minded – you can cast out as far as you would wish to or even as far as you can. By now there is less harm in scaring the fish. Your line may well have been over them. If they have seen the nymph – and a trout's eyesight is very keen – then it has been refused.

You have spent about half an hour now searching the water. Your concentration is not as good as it was – though you do not realize it – and you are casting a longer way out. The nymph is fishing quite deep, perhaps three or four feet down, and as you start a slow draw to bring it to the surface the floating nylon seems to halt for a moment in the water. That is a take and you missed it. You were too slow.

Sometimes a take will come so gently that all you will see will be this slight check to the movement of the nylon. The sign is sometimes so slight that unless you are concentrating very hard you will be unaware of what has happened. Trout take the nymph very gently when it is fished sub-surface – especially when it is fished slowly – and if it so happens the direction of the take is in the same direction as the retrieve you may never see it at all. If it is at right angles to the direction of the retrieve one can perhaps hope for a little more than a slight check on the line but not much more. Only if the trout takes against the direction of the retrieve are you likely to see the nylon drawing under sharply – going through the hole in the water – as it does every time in a take on a river.

Smash takes, as they are called – a great bang on the line as the fish takes the fly – do not occur in sub-surface nymph fishing, only sometimes in deep-sunk nymph fishing when one is using the technique of the induced take. You cannot use the induced take in calm water – at least not to any appreciable extent. I no longer try. It causes too much disturbance.

When a trout takes the nymph it does so very gently, and as soon as he feels the hardness of the hook under the body he ejects it like lightning. So you have very little time to set the hook home. I once watched the whole process in the clear chalk-stream waters of Dermot Wilson's pool at Nether Wallop. A boy was fishing the nymph. He would throw the line and the nymph would sink slightly below the surface. Then he would draw, very slowly, and you watched and waited. If the path of the nymph and the path of a cruising trout coincided it became very exciting. You would see the trout deflect very slightly from his path – they never chased the nymph – and pick it up in his mouth as he passed. You could see the white line of the mouth as it opened. Almost at once – almost a milli-second of time later – you would see the mouth open again and you would know the nymph had been rejected. Sometimes there was no movement of the nylon on the surface at all, sometimes only a momentary check to the retrieve.

You see what I mean about nymph fishing being delicate?

I remember that at the time I kept a record of the number of takes we had observed from our vantage point above the water. There were about a dozen. But the angler was lower than we were and the light on the water was against him so that he could only tell that he had a take by the movement either of the nylon or the line. He thought he had had only one or two takes – and he had missed them all. Mind you – he was a beginner. But the fact was that the majority of takes were not registered by any movement of the line.

Eventually he caught a trout which we had seen about to take the nymph and so we shouted out to him 'Strike!' a fraction of a second before the trout took. The strike came at the exact moment the fish had the nymph in his mouth.

It was an exciting and illuminating experience. It taught me one very important rule about nymph fishing. When, in calm conditions, you are fishing the nymph very slowly – as indeed you must – do not let it sink too deep or the takes will not be seen. Fish it as near to the surface as you possibly can. The deeper the nymph the faster it has to be fished in order to make sure that at least some of the takes are seen by the movement or checking of the nylon on the surface.

Well – now you have seen how the fish take the nymph and now you know that you have to strike – or rather tighten into the fish – at the slightest check of the nylon. The concentration has to be very intense indeed. I once took a friend nymph fishing and watched him miss five takes in succession – either because he was not concentrating sufficiently hard or else his reactions were too slow. He did not take a fish until I gave him a lure and told him to fish it fast.

As you begin to fish again a slight wind ripples the surface of the water. Now you have a better chance because you can try the induced take. Your nymph is out about ten yards from the bank and has sunk two or three feet down in the water. Let it sink. Do not move the nymph at all for a moment.

Imagine to yourself the nymph is down there, not very far perhaps from a weed bed, and it has been disturbed or alarmed by a trout searching among the weeds. It is

Flies and Nymphs

Compared with the gaudy dressings of lures and wet-flies, the true lake patterns copy the colours of the natural insect and are of about the same size. There are many dressings of which these are only a few. The palmer nymph is second from the left in the second row, next to one of C. F. Walker's patterns, to show the similarity in colouring.

The dry flies at the top are: a Greenwell, which represents most of the duns; a red palmer, which is a good suggestion of the sedge flies; and John Goddard's tying of an olive spinner which is fished in the surface film when spent flies are on the water.

The distinctive green and brown nymph on the right of the second row is a pattern widely used at Two Lakes and is heavily leaded at the thorax to sink quickly. Next to it is John Goddard's nymph dressing which uses olive-coloured condor herl covered with olive-coloured plastic – hence the name PVC nymph.

A nymph and a dry fly, in various sizes, chosen from these patterns will be enough for most waters but three pupae have also been included (bottom row) as an example of the many imitations of natural insects that can be used. They are Goddard's red midge; a useful sedge pupa by C. F. Walker; and a small black midge which in larger sizes is similar to a Blagdon pattern known as The Buzzer, which was invented by Dr Bell of Wrington.

PLATE V

Palmer Nymphs Under Water

A trout's view of the palmer nymph as it passes through water in varied conditions of light and background. Under some conditions the bright golden-olive colours are darkened considerably so that the nymph appears little more than a drab olive silhouette with a large part of the hackling almost invisible. A moment later some of the colours reappear and the hackling becomes more distinct. There is also a subtle change of colour in the hackles, according to the amount of and the angle of the reflected light. It is all these characteristics, taken together, as the nymph moves through the water, which – it is suggested – help to create the illusion that the creature is alive and has an "inbuilt movement" of its own. The nymph in all these pictures is the same. It was tied on a size 10 hook and attached to a length of 5 lb breaking strain nylon. The photographs were taken by John Lawton.

very alarmed. It darts away several feet, very quickly, then it stops and rests.

You visualize this happening and suddenly you draw the line sharply down with your left hand as far as it can go. You stop there and wait. That has given the nymph the sudden movement of alarm.

Remember that rapid movement should only be given to the nymph in rippled water. In calm water movement should be gentle. In calm water and bright sunshine there are the hazards both of line wake and the shadow cast by the nylon and the line. The greater the disturbance the less likely the trout is to take. In water with strong waves try drifting the nymph with the wind, pulling it gently across the waves. Try one or two induced takes and then bring the nymph in gently so that you can see it come to the surface before lifting off for the next cast.

Try and make it appear that the nymph has darted up from a weed bed, in a slightly zig-zag course, until it has slowed down close to the surface. One never knows when a take will come – sometimes during the long quick pulls, sometimes in the pauses in between, and sometimes a trout will follow the nymph right in to the side and take it almost at your feet.

The ripple is still on the water so you can try again. Cast a little farther so that you search fresh water that has not been lined. Let the nymph sink well.

Try a straight retrieve this time. Keep the point of your rod low, pointing towards the nymph. This is keeping what we call a tight line – no belly in the line between you and the nymph – so that if you see a take you lift the rod quickly and lose no time in tightening on to the fish. The nymph has gone well down. Take the line in your left hand and concentrate. Imagine that you are a water creature which has suddenly taken alarm and needs to escape from imminent danger. You pull the line sharply, almost as far as you can reach, pushing the left hand down to your side. The sinking nymph will suddenly accelerate towards the surface.

Nothing happens. The line is still tight because it is held against the rod by the fingers of the right hand, where it is held between your first and second fingers. Release the grip on the line with your left hand and slowly, very slowly, bring your left hand up to the rod again until it takes a new grip on the line just by your right hand.

An alarmed nymph! Your left hand goes right down again to your side, pulling in almost another yard of line. If a trout sees the sudden acceleration of the nymph he may well chase and take.

No – nothing happens.

But what is that? The line has stopped moving through the water and is now almost at rest but there is something queer about it. If you had not been watching the line carefully you would have missed it. It was hardly a pull – just a slight deflection of the line in the ripple – but your nerves were tensed and you lifted the rod. As you did so you felt the fish.

One knows from experience what happens. A trout will see the sudden movement – the flash of an alarmed creature – and providing the nymph does not move too quickly out of his vision he will rise and take, selecting this particular insect out of many because it attracted him by the movement and then remained within reach. Always give the trout a chance to follow the nymph. If you pull continuously or too fast it is likely that the fish will not bother to waste the energy on chasing such a small creature. The fast movement attracts the trout, possibly arouses its hunting instinct, and then suddenly the nymph slows down and appears to be an easy prey.

Sometimes of course the trout will take during the fast retrieve and in such cases may well be felt before the pull on the nylon is seen. Very often the take will be in between the fast movements. Each take is different. You never know when or how it will come. Sometimes if you pull at the moment the fish takes you will feel the fish before the line has moved. Sometimes the take will be quite a violent movement of the nylon and the cast – they will slide away from you for several feet. At other times there will be hardly a movement. This is when you say you strike 'by instinct'.

This fish is a good one. He is taking you all over the pool. As he is making his first turn and the line is cutting through the water, he changes direction. The line is still going in one direction but the fish leaps in another and crosses back under your line. Walk back a little to keep the line tight while you retrieve the loose line by hand. Keep in contact. Play him by hand while the first fury is on. He is making another rush and all the loose line is going after him. Now you can play him from the reel. Keep the point of the rod high so that he tires against the spring of the rod. Play him off the check. Let him take line if he wants to. This is a good-sized fish and these first runs are very powerful.

He is tiring and coming in. Gently now. Keep up the pressure. He is off again as soon as he is near the bank. But now you are bringing him in again and he is turning over on his side. Glide him in over the net. He is yours! A lovely shasta rainbow that will go all of two and a half pounds and in the pink of condition.

VII

Fishing the Rise—Casting Short—Going for a Cruiser

So far we have seen how to fish the sub-surface nymph in a flat calm and how to change our tactics when the breeze suddenly puts a ripple on the water. But we have not, as yet, cast to rising fish.

A rise is when the trout breaks the surface of the water and the rings spread outwards – a most invigorating sight which is often quite enough to make the heart beat faster and the hand lose its cunning. Various writers – Ivens and Goddard and others – have given very good advice on fishing the rise: to drop your fly into the rings as soon as possible or to cast ahead of the fish in the direction in which he is travelling.

If you know.

If – like me – you often have very little idea which way the fish is going then you will not be able to drop the nymph in front of it at a reasonable distance away and as trout do not necessarily travel up-wind all the time you may put your fly a quite unreasonable distance behind him by mistake. I have found it no bad plan to compromise and cast slightly short of the rise — directly to it but slightly short. This may be no more effective than casting to the left or the right of the rise but the one advantage it has is that you are less likely to line the fish. If the trout is still somewhere within the area of the rise he should – at least in theory – see the nymph but not the nylon.

But one of the most difficult problems to solve is that of the size of your nymph. I remember one day at Blagdon when I saw one or two rises by a weed bed, fairly close in, in shallow water. I stooped down and worked myself into a position where I could see fairly clearly into the water though at that moment the fish was not visible. But soon I saw a rise so I cast short in the direction of the rise, about a yard from the weed bed. The trout came out at once, quite quickly, approached the nymph and turned away in disgust. There was no question of a take. He knew it was not food, or was it selective feeding? I have no idea. So I changed from the large nymph I was using (size 10) to a small one (size 14) and cast again. It fell in the same place and the trout came out again and this time took with confidence. I did not land him because in those days I had a passion for fishing fine – dear me, the mistakes I have made! – and he turned in to the weeds and that was the end. I would no longer fish with 2 lb breaking strain casts at Blagdon because it is asking for trouble. Three pounds will do but four is better and as for me I am happy with five.

Then, of course, the reverse sometimes happens. A trout will ignore tiny nymphs and go for the big ones, though this generally happens when you are fishing deep. Then they will sometimes take size 10 or even 8 and disregard anything smaller. I have a number of theories about this. Every angler has theories. I speculate that perhaps trout have no definitions on sizes, have no capacity for putting them into categories, but are merely alarmed by other and unknown factors. It may be something to do with selective feeding. Lakes are full of nymphs – for example, the demoiselles – which are much larger than those we normally tie. Whatever the answer, in practice it means that though you do not need to change your pattern you do need to change your size.

Fishing the rise is full of interest. No rise pattern seems to be always quite the same, and no take seems to be the same. Each – as Howard Marshall puts it – is a unique event. It sometimes happens, on certain lakes, that if you cast to the rise and then leave the fly in that area, moving it gently, it is taken long after the fish has passed. In these cases it may be other trout following in the path of the first, or possibly the original trout which has cruised round in a circle and re-entered the same area of water because the hatch of nymph there is more numerous than in other parts of the lake. If I see a rise, cast to it, and get no response, I will continue casting to the same area – slightly short of where the rise was – for some ten minutes or so and if after that time there are no further rises in that place I may discontinue. But I would not have you give up too easily. Where a trout has been once, he may come back, or another may follow.

Indeed there are some trout which seem to have the habit of cruising in circles over a well-defined area, which – possibly – they have mapped out in their own minds as their domain. If there is good weed cover and the insects are prolific in numbers he may circle gently for a long time, picking one up here and there as he goes; and one must remember that for every take that shows on the surface there must be many more which do not show at all. So if one must make a rule about fishing the rise then it is that one should persist to fish to it for some time and if need be alter the size of your hook before departing elsewhere.

And now we come to the question of sticklebackers – those large trout that chase the shoals of small fry into the shallows on August evenings. This is where the lure fisherman, of course, comes into his own, or at least is very confident that he does. I did well enough with Grandpa Cox's minnow fly and with the Dunkeld at Blagdon and Weir Wood in the old days but I also did quite well with an Invicta and a Black Pennell, and these can hardly be said to be imitations of small fish. The truth is that sticklebacking trout are not quite so selective as some would have us believe. I do not think my nymphs look like tiny fish so what the sticklebacker takes them for I do not know. But take them he does. Time and time again I have been forced to the conclusion that even when trout appear to be feeding selectively they will take a properly-presented nymph.

Presentation is of such enormous importance that I must be forgiven if I emphasize again and again that no matter how perfect your pattern of nymph if you present it badly it will not be taken. You can judge for yourself on those occasions when you see and cast to a cruising fish.

This, to me, is one of the most delicate and skilful aspects of lake fishing – exemplified perhaps by the story of one of the rods at Two Lakes who is said to have the most acute under-water vision and the most astonishing ability to make himself invisible. This apocryphal character is said to haunt the rhododendron bushes of the Home Pool but because of his camouflaged clothing and almost total immobility no one is aware of his presence without a careful search of the undergrowth, and sometimes not even then. He is reputed to have the ability to stand there for several hours at a time, without casting, almost without breathing, until he sees the trout he wants – he will take nothing under three pounds. He will then drop a nymph soundlessly and delicately in front of the fish, which invariably takes it. If it does not, he loses patience and shoots it.

I am not in the category of grand master. My underwater vision is poor, my casting less accurate than it should be, and although I do make some attempt to be unseen I am all too often aware that I have blundered. This is why, if possible, I like to cast on this side of the fish – so that he sees as little as possible of the nylon – and to cast in such a way that he is not alarmed by the sudden arrival of a nymph on his nose. There may be some delicate way of putting a nymph on top of a trout, or within a foot or so, in such a way that he regards it as the natural arrival of an edible creature – and if caterpillars are dropping from trees that may be one such – but on the whole I have found that if I cast too close to the fish he will certainly inspect it but almost as certainly refuse it. This, I take it, is because the trout is sufficiently aware that a nymph does not normally arrive from the sky.

The trout's eyesight is very keen – we have all of us had the experience of how they will rise to a knot in the nylon cast – and I have had them take my nymph even when I have dropped it six to nine feet away. If it is cast this far away they are not, I assume, aware that something has dropped from the sky, more that something has made a disturbance in the water – the kind of disturbance, for example, that a nymph might well make if it is struggling to free itself from the shuck. They will cruise up and see the nymph still on the surface – in which case the hackles will be glinting as though they they are the emergent wings – or just below the surface when as like as not the air bubbles will still be surrounding the hackles with an aura of silver, and if this appears to them to be in the natural order of things they will take.

But each case is different.

There is no fixed routine in fishing the nymph that can be applied to each and every occasion. If there were, it would be dull indeed, there would be no problems to solve, no sense of triumph, no achievement. It would become as routine a matter as using a spinner – feathered or otherwise.

Consider the problems we had with the biggest rainbow I ever caught.

This was a very big rainbow, in Dermot Wilson's pool at Nether Wallop. We could see him cruising and both my son and I had tried for him and failed. I do not know how many times we had failed to persuade him to take – ten perhaps or maybe twenty – but it had seemed to go on for a large part of the afternoon.

He was an enormous fellow and clearly visible from our vantage point on a fairly high grassy bank whenever he came into view – and I daresay we were clearly visible to him too at the same time which was a good deal of the trouble. He was cruising very slowly round and round the pool in a clearly defined pattern. We had to wait for him to come round and then for eight or ten yards or so he was visible as he circled and then he disappeared under a patch of ruffled water, went out of sight, and then reappeared some five or six minutes later. There was no doubt it was the same fish – the biggest in sight – and one with a most disdainful expression.

We carried out the usual routine. We left the nymph waiting for him and did an induced take in front of him. We dropped it to one side and twitched it past. We even dropped it on his nose. He never even turned to look. This – if there ever was one – was an educated fish, or what we like to call an educated fish.

Eventually it dawned upon me that we could be seen. It was true we were taking some sort of cover, but obviously not enough. I did not think he was a 'selective feeder' and in this I was right because when he was eventually caught he was packed full of snail but even so he took a nymph when it was properly presented.

But what was the proper way to present a nymph to this dreadfully arrogant-looking monster of a trout?

I suppose if we were really intelligent fishermen it would have been or should have been obvious to begin with, but when you see a fish of that size cruising within reach you become excited and throw the fly at it on the assumption the fish will play, and he did not. Eventually it dawned on me that so long as we could see the fish and he could see us there was no possibility of a take; and as we were on an exposed grassy bank with the sky behind us I doubt very much if it would have made any difference if we had lain flat on our faces. The grass was as short as a crew-cut and sloped right down to the water's edge without a hummock or a rush in sight.

So we had to stamp on our enthusiasm and use our intelligence. The nymph had to be presented to the trout after he had passed us, or before he got to us, but certainly not while we were in view. The best way would be to present the nymph to the trout while he was moving away from us – while he had his back turned – because he would then not be likely to associate us with the little creature that was rising from the bed of the lake in front of him after he had left us out of sight behind.

This was the theory.

So, when the trout passed, we would have to throw the nymph behind him to the ruffled patch of water some ten or twelve yards away to his left. He would then gradually circle round and enter this ruffled patch of water, by which time he would have his tail to us and the sight of us would also be obscured by the ruffled surface. We would then estimate the time of his arrival and the place of his arrival and we would give an induced take to the nymph, which by that time would be well sunk down in the water, perhaps three or four feet down or more, and hopefully not too far away from him.

Remember, this was the same nymph that he had seen a dozen or maybe two dozen times and in which he had not shown the slightest interest. Yet, on the second or third cast to the ruffled water, he took it with complete confidence and because he was moving away from us the nylon drew down sharply.

A fraction of a second before it drew I had exclaimed 'I think he's gone past' because I thought the induced take must have been ignored, but it came as I spoke. When I tightened it felt like a salmon.

He surfaced in a turmoil of water, coming up slowly with a great bow wave in front of him, the water peeling over like the earth tumbling from the cutting share of a plough, first the huge head showing and then the long, long flanks, pink and golden and shining, never seeming to end, and finally the dark and monstrous thickness of the tail. I was weak in my legs at the sight of him but he seemed to give up after the first heavy pull and the only real difficulty we had with him was to get him in the net.

'That is something like a fish,' says Dermot respectfully when he sees him, and fetches the camera. It was a rainbow and within three ounces of the record of those days, turning 8 lb 5½ ozs on the Nether Wallop butchers' scales, with a girth of 18 inches and a length from nose to fork of 26.

Since then I use a larger net.

I remember that it took me some time to adjust to the fact that I had caught a trout several pounds heavier than any I had ever caught before. One needs a period of adjustment to the experience of a lifetime. Even when my son and I drove off to Blagdon the next day I remember suddenly bursting out aloud in my excitement:

'Eight pounds five and a half ounces!'

'There, there!' said my son, soothingly.

'But Nicholas – eight pounds five and a *half* ounces!'

The half ounce, for some reason, seemed to be of enormous importance.

'Yes, father. There, there! It's all right!'

It took me a long time to recover.

The main lesson that one can learn as a nymph fisherman – once again – is that the capture of each cruising fish is a separate and unique event. The approach, the tactics and the method of the final capture depend upon a multitude of circumstances and conditions which are not static, which are varying all the time, which create innumerable problems, none of which may be immediately evident or understood except perhaps in retrospect – when it may be too late.

The only guideline one has is that the nymph must be presented to the trout in such a way that it does not arouse suspicion. If the trout is hungry – and cruising trout are generally looking for food – and if no extraneous events occur which are suspicious or alarming then the likelihood is that the nymph will be taken. But there are a thousand things which will prevent a take – the glint of nylon, a thud on the bank, the flash of sunlight from the rod as it makes the cast – the list is endless.

One is continually forced into an appraisal of problems. This – so it seems to me – is the charm of fishing the nymph. One sets out deliberately to suggest the movement of a particular creature – one of the trout's staple forms of food – and one almost forces the trout into a situation where he will be so deceived by your skill and by your presentation of the nymph that it will be more natural for him to take it than to refuse.

To say this is apparently to suggest that a take is

almost inevitable providing the presentation is correct. Let us perhaps put it another way. When my nymph has been refused I can generally work out why it has been refused and the reasons are invariably bad presentation of one kind or another, even if I only discover them too late. On some lakes one only has one chance before the fish may be out of range and in these circumstances the presentation must be right first time – and I have an inbuilt capacity for doing the wrong thing, especially in a hurry.

There are times of course when fish simply will not feed at all. We all know them. If the stock fish are disinclined to take their liver pellets then one can shrug one's shoulders and put the rod up for a while. Perhaps the air is too full of static, perhaps the air pressure is too high, perhaps the oxygen content of the water is too low – there are such occasions during a season which are a part of our experience. There are such days. But they are infrequent. We must not use them as an excuse.

Most of us have to admit to failure on more occasions than we like. I remember one morning at Two Lakes casting to persistent risers for several hours without a single touch. It only occurred to me over lunch that what I had not tried was to change the size of my nymph. It was simply that my intelligence was not working well. I had been fishing without thinking. It happens to everyone. By the time I went back to the lake with a smaller nymph the fish had stopped rising. It is good for the soul to make mistakes. It keeps one humble.

It is also best to fish alone.

Though perhaps it is not unwise to have a companion somewhere in case of need. There is the gruesome story of how a man went exploring round the shores of a loch in the remote Western Highlands and found the skeleton of an angler lying as he had fallen on the rocks of the shore. The skeleton was still clasping a rod in its hands and the line was still in the water so the man disengaged the rod from the grasp of the skeletal fingers and carefully wound in the line and on the end of it was the skeleton of a fish.

So there are times, also, when it is not good to fish too much alone.

VIII

Fishing Deep—Large Nymphs—A Day at the End of the Season

THERE are times when it is useful to use a large nymph, with six to eight turns of lead wire round the thorax under the dubbing, on a number 8 hook. When is it necessary? The answer is when the trout are lying deep and refusing to rise to the sub-surface nymph.

I realize that is not a very satisfactory answer – it is not very precise and it is not very clear and it is rather an obvious generalization. But – as will be quite clear from an example given later on in this chapter – one should not be too precise or too didactic about our methods.

There are certain signs which may guide you into using a deep-sunk nymph but they are by no means infallible. All lakes are different. Every day is different. The hours of the day are different. One must make a judgement according to one's experience of the lake and one's observation of conditions.

If there is a sign anywhere of a fish moving or rising then it will mean there are trout in the upper levels of water – not deeper than four or five feet – and in these circumstances the sub-surface nymph is by far the most productive and pleasant method. The nymph can be fished slowly and delicately and a higher proportion of takes will be registered on either the floating nylon or the floating line.

But there are some days – and especially on large lakes – when there is no sign of a fish at all and when it is likely that most or all of the fish are lying deep, well off shore, possibly feeding on insects in the mud or off weed beds which are perhaps eight or ten feet down and sometimes much deeper than that. These are the days when many reservoir anglers scrape the bottom in twenty or thirty feet of water, using very large lures, long leaders and sinking lines.

This is not very interesting fishing.

If one has to fish the nymph in such circumstances then it will have to be fished fast to register a take. The technique is more or less the same as ordinary wet-fly fishing – a long cast, a long pause to allow the nymph to get well down, and then a fairly fast jerky retrieve. If one is using a sinking line then the take will be felt rather than seen. In such circumstances the nymph has little advantage over any other method.

So even if I fish the nymph deep I still use a floating line but with a very long leader – one of perhaps 15 or 16 feet. These are difficult to cast but the advantage is that the take can still be registered on the floating line even though on some occasions the line tip will itself begin to sink owing to the combined weight of the nymph and the sunken cast.

A general rule would be that the deeper the nymph the faster it has to be fished in order that the take can either be observed on the surface or felt as a direct contact. There are times – though not many – when I do fish a nymph deeply, anywhere between about six feet to twelve feet down. But the deeper I go the more I find that I lose touch, the more coarse and fast becomes the retrieve, and the delicate quality of fishing the nymph is gradually lost.

But how often is deep-nymph fishing really necessary?

At one time I used to fish much deeper than I do now. This, I suspect, was a residual habit from my wet-fly and lure days, from the attitude of mind which automatically prompts you to 'get down to the fish' on the assumption that if you cannot see a rise the fish must be lying deep. Sometimes this must be so – as when there is a school of rainbow lying deep under the dam at Blagdon, for example – and boat anglers with sinking lines do very well. But in my own experience I do not think it occurs so frequently that it excludes all other methods. Even if many fish are taking deep there are still many other fish exploring the margins which will rise to a nymph that is perhaps somewhere between four and eight feet down.

During the last three seasons, therefore, I have given up using 15 ft leaders in favour of the 12 ft leader, leaving the whole length of it ungreased. I use a heavy leaded nymph – a size 8 – and allow it to sink well. Sometimes I will begin my retrieve when the leader is only half sunk. Sometimes I will wait for the entire length of the leader to sink before beginning the retrieve. By this method the nymph can be fished at varying levels – possibly the deepest being about eight or nine feet down.

This seems to me to be a reasonable compromise. But it is not a delicate method and there are many drawbacks. The hook is large and hard and the rejection is probably almost instantaneous so that there are many takes which will be missed, unless the nymph is being moved fast at the moment of impact. One loses the advantage of a delicate entry to the water and line wake is appreciable so that the method cannot be used very satisfactorily in calm water. I would not, however, rule out the possibility that there are times when a deep-sunk nymph is necessary to take fish. But I would on the whole keep this method as a last resort when all the possibilities of the sub-surface nymph have been exhausted.

During the last three seasons most of my trout have been taken on the sub-surface nymph – that is to say a nymph on a greased cast fished at levels varying from an inch or so below the surface to somewhere between three and four feet below – the latter depth being the extreme limit of the fishing – with an average depth of between two and three feet. For this kind of fishing one does not need a nymph heavier than a number 10 – either loaded with lead or copper wire – and I would normally use a size 12.

It is a fallacy that a large bait is always needed for a large fish. Most of my biggest fish have been taken on quite small nymphs – on 10, 12 or 14 hooks – and the reason for this is simply that a small nymph is more or less the same size as the real thing, looks so much more natural in the water, and responds so much more realistically to the movements imparted to it during the retrieve. And I suppose one could add that the hook is much less visible.

The stomachs of some of the biggest trout – four and five pounders – are sometimes crammed with midge and nymph, none of which are much longer than the diameter of a half-penny coin.

Come down to the lake again and see what we can learn on a day when, quite deliberately, we start off using a deep-sunk nymph. Let us take a day in late September, in fact the last fishing day of the season, at a time of the year when the trout – in John Goddard's words – 'are wary and difficult to catch'.

Let us go to a larger lake this time – a four or five acre water – where the lure fishermen have been busy for nearly six months without ceasing and the water has been flogged and lined from all quarters.

The clouds are heavy. There is a spattering of rain. The water is low after drought and the ribs of the banks are showing. The water is speckled brown and gold with fallen leaves. There is a cold nip in the air and the wind is ruffling – it is what Pooh would have called a blustery sort of a day.

We arrive late for some reason or other – I think it was because I had to call and collect you at your house – so by the time we have parked the car and assembled the rods it is nearly noon. We stand and look at the Home Pool for a while but there is not a sign of anything moving at all so we wander round to find out what has been happening. Up under the pine trees at Border pool a lure fisherman has been working steadily for three hours without a touch. The neat little dry-fly lady is looking philosophic and sending her husband back to the car to get a thermos of tea. Conditions are said to be 'dour' though there is a rumour that someone, somewhere, has had a fish, but it is not known how or on what.

So I say that we might as well try the deep nymph. This, as it happens, is a mistake and I should have known better but we all of us make mistakes and this is one of them. It is true that I have an excuse – it is cold and blustery and no fish are showing at all – but all the same it was a mistake.

You put on a heavy nymph on an ungreased cast – a size 8 – and we begin on the Lower Lake where the waves are tumbling and the wind blowing. You move along the banks, searching the water, giving the nymph as much variety of movement as possible but letting it sink well down before beginning the retrieve. Then you bring it to the surface fast, with three or four sharp pulls, then let it hover and sink down a little, then another sharp pull to try and induce a trout to take.

You start by casting along the bank – a cast of no more than ten or twelve yards which drops the nymph a few yards only from the shore. Then you cast farther out so that it drops five yards from the shore, then ten yards, and eventually you cast straight out at an angle of ninety degrees from the shore, first of all ten or twelve yards out, then fourteen or fifteen, then fifteen to twenty, so that the nymph is fishing fresh unlined water all the time.

You vary the retrieve as much as possible but the water is rough and the takes will be difficult to see so that you can hardly stroke the water as in sub-surface fishing and you have to move the nymph faster. Sometimes try and not let the nymph sink too deep. When it is only a foot or so below the surface you can try a slower retrieve, moving it very gently, then allowing it to sink, then suddenly accelerating it. By this means you can explore various levels of water at various speeds – slow, moderate, fast – never allowing your concentration to relax, always trying something new. You are searching for invisible fish which may be feeding at any depth. When you have fished out one patch of water move gently and quietly on to the next.

Give the other rods a wide berth. Most of them will be fishing one particular area of water, remaining in one place for some time, generally casting out as far as they can. There are in fact several of them bunched fairly close together on one bank with the wind behind them. That is the bank to avoid. Go past and fish the unlined and undisturbed water on the other side. Casting may be more difficult. No matter. A nymph fisherman must learn to cast across and into the wind.

All the same, as you move gradually round the lake and come head on into the wind the going is not easy. Nearly two hours have gone by and nothing has happened – not a touch and not a sign of a fish moving. You are out on a small narrow stretch of land now with shallow water on one side and deep water on the other and you have fanned your casts all round, deep and shallow, fast and slow, putting everything you know into working the nymph in as lifelike a fashion as you can. But there has not been a touch. The wind is blowing hard in your face and you are casting badly. The nymph is not turning over well and sometimes the leader will land on the water in curls and circles of nylon and sometimes the nylon will curl over itself in the air. This is the time when the nymph will go through a loop of the nylon and before you know what has happened will tie a knot in it by itself. Wind knots, they're called, and very dangerous they are. If you take a big fish with a wind knot in your leader you are likely to break at the knot – the nylon seems to cut into itself very deeply and quickly and under any strain the leader will break. Every now and again run your fingers down the whole length of your leader to make sure there are no wind knots in it. If there are, you have to pick the knot apart, using the point of a pin. On a bad day you can pick up a couple of wind knots in as many minutes, especially if you are trying to cast too far. If you think that the wind knots have weakened the nylon there is nothing for it but to put on a new point.

It is hard going.

If you have ever thought that Two Lakes is easy fishing then a day like this will teach you otherwise. Nearly three hours now and not a sign of anything at all. This is the danger period. You are beginning to cast automatically, pulling in automatically, losing concentration. The best thing we can do, having nearly fished the lake round, is to have a breather, go back to the car, have a cup of tea, a swig from the whisky flask, and a Marmite sandwich. It may sound spartan fare but a Marmite sandwich has a good hard taste to it and a drop of whisky keeps away evil. So – yes – let us improve our morale and go back to the car for ten minutes or so and think things over.

You have one last cast – far out this time and a fairly quick and thoughtless retrieve but you are still sensible enough to fish out your cast, bringing the nymph right into the side and right up to the surface before lifting off – and just as the nymph comes to the surface a yard or so from the bank a trout swirls at it. You feel nothing and see nothing except the slight boil in the water as the fish turns away and that is all.

Well – at least the fish are there!

No – don't start flogging the water in the hope that the fish will come again. It may do but as like as not it won't. It did, after all, refuse to take even though it had followed the nymph in, perhaps for a foot or so, perhaps for longer. One can't say. But the evidence is of a refusal, not of a take, and that is evidence which must be considered rather carefully.

Let us think it over with the whisky and the Marmite sandwiches.

Remember the man fishing the deep lure up at the Border pool? You remember seeing the rods we passed as we went round the lake? I do not know what they were using but most of them were fishing well down in the water. So, as likely as not, most of the men who have been fishing have been using rather large flies. Our own rather large nymph has been followed but refused.

And – remember – the refusal came just below the surface close in to the side.

Why on earth didn't we think of it in the first place? I don't know. But it is quite clear what you must do.

You cut off the large nymph and put on a smaller nymph – a size 12 – which is also less heavy and will not sink so deep and you grease your cast down to the last foot or so. Now you will be fishing only a few inches down or a foot or so down at the most.

The evidence, or what we have of it, is fairly clear. The trout are disinterested in large flies and in flies fished deep. So – one puts on a smaller fly and fishes it higher in the water. It sounds very simple – yet in fact we have been fishing for nearly three hours without thinking of it, without even suspecting it as a possibility.

Let us take a little more whisky to revive our morale and start again.

This time – and I am writing this from my records – we are in luck. Just by chance as we are passing the dog's leg end of the Home Pool I happen to see a slight hump in the water. That is the first sign of a fish moving that we have seen. There is no time to waste. But it is a devil of a place to put a nymph as the water is speckled with floating autumn leaves. Kneel down now and cast towards the place where the hump in the water showed us the fish was moving, cast a little short so as not to disturb him, and if you hook a leaf do not try and whip it off your hook because that will scare the trout sick – just draw it in gently to the side and remove it by hand.

The first cast you get a leaf. But keep on trying. There is a fish out there somewhere and if you have not lined him there may be a chance. Gently now. Move the nymph very very slowly, a foot or so every five seconds and no more, glide it along very gently a few inches below the surface. The light is bad. You cannot see the nylon, only the slow gliding white line. Quite softly and slowly the line appears to hesitate for a moment in the middle of a glide and that is the moment when you tighten in to your fish. You feel it hard and heavy on the hook and the rod top bends but then suddenly all goes slack.

Now that is very odd.

Sometimes you will feel a pluck at your nymph and tighten and there will be nothing there, but in this case the fish was on and you knew that the hook had gone home – so either it had taken too shallow a hold on a thin sliver of tissue or else you were broken at the knot. For the moment you cannot think of any other reason.

Yet on this particular day there was another. The hook itself had broken.

But the fish are still moving – humping the water – so you tie on another number 12 nymph and begin again and in half an hour there is another take and you tighten and feel the fish and the line goes slack. It cannot happen again and yet it has – the hook has broken again just above the barb. I take out my plastic box and throw away all my size 12 nymphs and go back to the car where I have a reserve supply though on slightly smaller hooks – size 13 – and we curse the hook makers or metal fatigue or whatever gremlin is responsible and take another whisky to ward off evil and go back again to the same place.

Persistence is a virtue. The fish are still moving here, under the trees, between the floating leaves.

You have to kneel to keep out of the sight of the trout and you start again, fanning the water, first along the bank, then moving out. Suddenly there is a bulge on the far side, right under the trees. Lengthen your line at once and try to reach that area. Keep the nymph there as long as you can before beginning to draw it back, very slowly, very gently. You have a leaf. Draw it in very gently, remove the leaf and start again. On the third cast the nylon goes through a hole in the water and the trout makes 1 lb 8 oz. Something tells you that there are more fish still there and after resting the spot for a while you start again with the same technique in the same place. You are rewarded, though the next fish only makes 1 lb 4 oz. Now we move on to the Lower Lake – the lake we first fished without result.

Here is something! A definite rise under a willow tree close in to the bank, probably a trout taking insects that are being blown off the trees. A dry fly will do nicely but if you are to reach that fish there may not be time to change the fly. Run your fingers down the greased nylon and give the nymph a rub. It should float for five minutes or so like that. It is well hackled, remember, and greased hackles will support the weight of a 13 hook for a while, even if the hook is weighted.

A sideways cast under the willow from a kneeling position and the little fly floats superbly for only a few seconds before it is engulfed. I know what is going to happen and it does. You strike too quickly – on the sight of the rise – and pull the fly out of the trout's mouth. You should have waited for the movement of the nylon as the trout turned to go down.

Well, it is a sad business so far: two trout lost with broken hooks, and one lost because of a strike which was too quick and only two small fish in the bag. This is the luck of the game – and even if it is not it is best to say so – though it would be nice on our last day to get a sizeable fish.

And now all goes quiet. No one, as they say, is catching anything. The old hands talk wisely of atmospheric pressure and static electricity and thunderstorms and the de-oxygenation of the water, but the fact is that after another two hours with the nymph you are tired and have lost your concentration and it is time to rest for a moment on one of the seats by the water. Fortunately when I brought out the new batch of hooks

I brought the thermos and the whisky. We will sit and look for moving fish and console ourselves.

A water vole comes sniffing round our feet – or is it a rat? – and takes no notice of us until he looks up and catches my eye. We stare at each other for a moment and he rushes off. This reminds me to tell you never to leave a freshly-caught trout on the bank. I did once and came back and found it half-eaten by something or other – probably a rat.

Sitting on this same seat, I once saw a grass snake swimming across the lake, just the head showing above the water, and it looked particularly beautiful because the head was held in the shape and way in which the ancient Egyptians carved the asp on their funerary urns, the perfect handle-like shape of the ceremonial asp, repeated in a Hampshire grass snake.

Which reminds me, I say, that once on the River Tay I hit a bat in mid-air with the top of my rod while I was casting. The creature weaved a bit under the shock but it flew on. Its radar had not been working.

We both see it at the same time as we are talking – a long way out in the lake, a considerable way out in the lake, the length of a cricket pitch away, somewhere where the fast bowler would be passing the umpire – an enormous and very heavy and purposeful rise, over there, in the windblown tumbling water.

You have on a small nymph, lightly greased to float, and you know enough about nymph fishing to know that a small dry fly out there is not likely to be seen in those heavy tumbling waves. What you have to do is to get a nymph out there quickly that will sink six inches or more. You have no time to change your fly. What can you do?

The secret is dust shot – not the heavy shot that coarse fishermen use on the big quill floats – but the smallest split shot obtainable. I always carry a little box of these and in emergencies of this kind they are invaluable. It does not take more than a few seconds for you to bite the dust shot on the nylon just in front of the eye of the hook. Now your greased nymph will sink. Quickly – cover the rise!

The first cast is short, very short, and there is no time and no need to worry about disturbing the water. You are well out of the target area. Roll cast the line up into the air and back and out again, shooting more line, and this time the cast is a good one and the nylon and the nymph disappear into the waves somewhere near where the trout rose. A few seconds for it to sink and then a sharp pull – an induced take – and then another. Nothing happens but as you pull back to cast again the trout rises a second time, moving in the same area but slightly to the left.

The second cast drops within a few yards. Let the fish have time to see the nymph. Let it sink. If he is looking that way he may come to it. Then when the nymph has sunk, draw quickly with the left hand to bring it up to the surface. You are out of the area now. Roll the line out and lift again into the air and again cast and shoot. Good. Let the nymph sink. Let it sink deeper, a foot or more. Now animate. As you make the first long draw with your left hand you see the white line move slightly away from you through the waves, making a little track through the water. A good take. Strike hard at that distance. Bring the rod up and feel for the fish at the same time by drawing on the line in your left hand.

Beautifully done! This is a big one! You can feel, heavy and hard, the deep solid weight of him. Give him line and hold the rod up because a fish of this size could break you on the knot – even of 6 lb nylon. There is tremendous power here and you must treat him gently. Off he goes like a torpedo, the line stripping off the reel, down to the backing. Let him go!

You're slipping on the mud and you have your landing net caught up somewhere. You're getting flustered and excited. Who doesn't? But you're making a mistake – you're trying to net him while he is still fighting. There, I knew it! By some miracle he is still on and the nylon has held, but you had him in the net and he came out of it again and the leader went over the metal frame! He is still fighting! You are holding him too hard. Let him tire himself. You will not be able to net him properly until he slips over on his side –

But by some extraordinary chance you have done so though it was you who went over on your side to do it, slipping down on the mud, spraying up mud and water over yourself, but holding the net high with the fish struggling in the mesh. Mud is streaming off your clothes but no matter. You have the fish and when you put him on Alex Behrendt's scales he goes down as 3 lb 11 oz.

That is not a bad fish with which to end the season.

IX

Some Practical Heresies—Imitations and Suggestions—The Palmer Dressing

I keep a notebook in my car and all the events recorded in the last chapter were scribbled down within an hour or so of the fish being caught. Imagination takes over very quickly if you do not make a point of writing down what happened as near to the time it happened as possible. It is necessary to try and get down on paper reasonably quickly the main details. Sometimes it is difficult to remember even a few minutes after a fish has been taken whether you were retrieving fast or slowly when the take came. Try it next time you land a fish and see if you can recall exactly what you were doing the moment before.

But that last day of the season was notable for many things that, seen in retrospect, are especially significant. There was the mistake about fishing deep, for example, and how it was discovered by a chance refusal close to the surface. With a little more intelligence one could have discovered this much earlier. Then there was the matter of the broken hooks. Two broken in a day when hooking fish is exceptional but looking back over my records I found that a total of nine hooks were broken on the take during that season. Perhaps I was unlucky to find so many bad-tempered hooks or perhaps – well, who knows what economies are now being made in the matter of mass-production?

But perhaps more significant for the nymph fisherman is the fact that this particular day showed how really versatile a nymph can be. The size 13 nymph took two fairly small fish just below the surface, fished slowly. A little grease transposed the same nymph into a 'dry' fly that floated long enough to rise a good fish under the willows; and not long afterwards the same fly, still greased but with a dust shot nipped in front of the eye, was cast some twenty yards to a rising fish which took it a foot or more below the surface of the waves. This is a pretty versatile performance.

Incidentally, there was an interesting point about that last fish – the one of 3 lb 11 oz. When I examined the stomach contents there was nothing in the stomach except a mass of white mucous-like material with small black specks in it. I could only assume it must be some form of plankton. One of the main food sources in some lakes is plankton crustaceae. I took it from the evidence – though there is no proof – that the two rises made by this trout before it took the nymph were swirls in the water made while it was cruising to take some of this plankton 'soup' just below the surface. It must be quite tasty stuff and it is therefore all the more encouraging – if my theory is correct – that a plankton-eating trout can be persuaded to turn aside to take a nymph.

And while we are speculating on such things it is right to remind you that Skues's marrow spoon is very useful to insert into a trout's stomach to find out what it has been feeding on. This is one of the things to carry with you. I daresay it is a heresy but I refuse to carry anything which cannot be put into my pockets. Fish light, whatever you do, and carry as little as possible.

For years I used to carry one of those large and

beautiful fishing bags but it became heavier and heavier and eventually I gave it up and left it in the boot of the car to hold my reserves. I now wear a fishing waistcoat under an army-surplus jacket which I bought for £2.50 in a shop in the Strand. The jacket is light and comfortable and has two large side pockets and two breast pockets. My equipment consists of two small plastic boxes of nymphs – one box containing weighted nymphs and the other unweighted, in various sizes, a tin and a bottle of floatant, a pair of scissors on a lanyard, a knife, a priest, a pair of small artery forceps for removing hooks, a small carborundum stone for sharpening hooks, one or two spools of nylon, a tube of anti-midge cream and one or two spare leaders, a box of dust shot, and – most important – several rather large pins stuck in the band of my fishing hat for undoing wind knots and taking the hard varnish out of the eyes of hooks.

I tie a length of ordinary quarter-inch nylon cord round my waist. My waterproof lightweight nylon trousers and fishing jacket can be folded over this cord, hanging down on either side, and pushed round at the back out of the way until needed. My landing net is also held by the cord, behind my back, with the net open and ready for use. I have experimented with other methods but these seem to me to be the most practical, though I must admit I look rather like a tramp with my net and waterproofs hanging from an old piece of rope. Nevertheless it works, and if I have to walk miles to get to my fishing then there is still room in my pockets for a packet of sandwiches and a hip flask and another piece of cord to loop on to the other on which I can thread my fish through the gills. One should, of course, carry a beautiful bag or creel and I would if I did not dislike the weight pulling on my shoulders – and if anyone made a creel big enough to carry a three-pounder without bending it in the middle. But that is enough about equipment – it is a subject on which everyone has his prejudices and of which most of us still carry too much.

Let us now consider the serious matter of the pattern of nymph that we should use.

Quite possibly we should have discussed it long before this because I have been talking cheerfully for some time on how to fish the nymph without describing what it is and what particular pattern I would recommend. The reason for this is not that I wanted to avoid discussing the dressing of nymphs – indeed I know that somewhere deep down I am a little inclined to be emotional upon the subject which is another reason for being cautious – but it is simply that the first priority in nymph fishing is to understand how to fish a nymph, almost any kind of nymph so long as it is a reasonable suggestion or imitation of the common underwater insect that goes by this name.

This, I know, is heresy so far as the angler-entomologists are concerned, but the actual technique of fishing is of paramount importance providing one uses a fly that is a reasonable suggestion of the nymph. There are, already, many reasonable suggestions and imitations on the market. Of the Ivens patterns, for example, there is the green and brown nymph, and both Walker and Goddard have good patterns as well, and I remember seeing a pattern designed by Michael Hordern for the rivers which looks as though it would take well on the lake, and then there are the Frank Sawyer patterns – all these have been designed by good practical fishermen with vast experience.

But if you are for any reason not as yet attached to any one of these – and I would not willingly unhook a man from his favourite fly – then we might go into the subject a little more deeply as, I assure you, it becomes more fascinating as we go along.

To begin with I believe it is important not to be led into the belief that it is necessary in any fly dressing to create an exact copy of the natural insect. I cannot do better on this subject than to quote the words of G. P. R. Pulman – the 'father of the dry fly' – who wrote in an article in *The Fisherman's Magazine and Review* of July, 1864:

> I have always found that a man who is for ever fretting himself about his flies has no reason to fret himself about the stowing away of his trout. Whilst he is disquieting himself in vain by catching natural flies – copying them, and catching nothing, his more sensible brother opposite fishes steadily on, not attempting to imitate that which it is impossible to imitate – the almost etherial forms of aquatic insects – but employing all his skill to present his fly-bait in such a manner that the fish mistake it for a thing endowed with life, rather than for the supposed 'copy' of something living. I am quite aware that this is not a new heresy. Neither is the imitation system a new fallacy.

This, I believe, is the right basis for the dressing of a nymph – that it should not necessarily 'copy' something living but should 'suggest something' that is endowed with life which is roughly or approximately of a nymphal shape and size. The pattern should be able to create an illusion of a nymph and the dressing should be such as to have a certain magic in its mixture so that when it is moved in the water it appears to come to life. It is for this reason that I have come to believe that the palmer-style dressing is the most effective in creating this illusion.

This – I must hasten to add – is not a discovery of my own. A palmer-dressed fly is not a new pattern. It is one of the oldest patterns of fly – possibly the oldest – that there is. In the year 1651 Thomas Barker wrote:

> Now to shew how to make Flies: learn to make two Flies, and make all; that is the Palmer, ribbed with silver or gold, and the May Flie; these are the grounds of all Flies.

Charles Cotton thought that the palmer 'did great execution' and Barker described it as a pattern which 'can be fished all the year long, morning and evening, windie and cloudie. . . .'

It is, of course, a method of dressing a fly rather than one particular pattern – a method by which hackle feathers are turned round the hook a number of times, reaching from the head of the fly to the middle of the shank or to the bend, thereby creating a bush or 'buzz' of hackle fibres.

Dressed thickly – that is with a thick buzz and the fibres close together all down the hook shank – the fly is sometimes said to suggest a 'woolly bear' caterpillar. Dressed more thinly, so that the body dubbing shows through, it can suggest a variety of insects – according to Courtney Williams it may well be taken for a shrimp, a nymph, or a number of types of larvae, and the large palmers fished on the surface 'are almost certainly taken for moths struggling on the water'.

A versatile dressing indeed!

The important thing to remember is the 'buzz' effect created by this method of hackling – an effect which no other form of fly dressing can possibly imitate and which is unique to the palmer method. The hundreds of fine delicate fibres standing out together, splayed out equally round the hook shank, catch and reflect the light which also shines through the fibres on to the dubbing. In certain conditions of light the sheer sparkle and translucence of this is quite dazzling and – what is equally important – the intensity and tone and quality of the light reflected changes with every movement of the fly as it passes the observer. This – I suggest – is why the palmer dressing has been so effective for so many years – it suggests a kind of movement within the fly itself.

As Skues wrote – 'the effect of fluttering and the effect of a bush of hackles may not look so dissimilar to the trout'.*

Now this, in my opinion, is what is missing from so many of the standard patterns of lake nymphs. They have a hard and almost rigid outline. The buzz effect, the illusion of movement, is missing.

Kingsmill Moore discovered this – or perhaps re-discovered it – some years ago when he created his Bumble patterns of flies – all of them palmer dressed. He wanted, he said, to construct a fly that would suggest the characteristics of underwater life:

> . . . it must be translucent, must have a certain amount of gleam without dazzle, must have gentle and not gaudy contrasts, and must if possible suggest the movement of an insect. . . .

That is to say the dressing must, within itself, create the illusion of an inbuilt movement, the flutter of legs perhaps or the rapid opening and closing of the gill plates along the sides of the nymph. The fluttering effect he wanted comes from the buzz of hackle.

We owe a great debt to Kingsmill Moore. His book – *A Man May Fish* – marks a significant stage in the art of dressing lake flies, especially in the technique he puts forward of mixed hackling. This gives a much more

* *The Way of a Trout with a Fly*. 4th Edn. p. 133

vivid impression of life and movement than the use of hackles of the same colour.

The technique is very simple. Two hackles – one, say, a dark red and the other a golden olive – are tied in together at the head of the fly. They are kept very tight and close together and wound together along the body of the fly down to the bend where they are secured and tied off. The red and golden-olive fibres of the hackles thus blend together in the tying and intermingle all the way down the body.

If such a mixed-hackle fly is held up to the light and turned gently from side to side the effect is remarkable. Sometimes the yellow-olive colour will predominate in the haze of hackles, sometimes the haze will be almost colourless – the 'sheer sparkle' described by Skues – and at other times there will be flashes of the red hackle and again at other times the colours will seem to blend together into a kind of orange tint. The dubbing on the body underneath adds its own translucency to the buzz effect. But – and this is very important – the spacing of the hackling must be right. Kingsmill Moore found that:

> . . . if the turns were too close the fly lost transparency, if too widely separated most of the life and brilliancy disappeared. Sometimes, if one colour were overpowering the other, half of the too-dominant hackle had to be stripped before it was tied on. The ideal fly looked rather bulky in the hand but lost all heaviness when viewed by transmitted light.

Kingsmill Moore was not concerned with suggesting a nymph, or indeed any particular kind of insect, merely to produce a fly dressing that created the illusion of life. His basic principle was based on the Derbyshire 'Bumbles' – which some say incidentally should be called

Yorkshire Bumbles – which are palmer-dressed flies of ancient lineage. Kingsmill Moore's own Bumbles were used mainly for sea trout – the white trout – of Irish lakes. He fished often from a boat and it is clear that he was not particularly concerned to imitate a nymph as such.

What was important for me when I read his book was its reminder of the value of the palmer dressing, and the possibility that the palmer dressing was the only one that could possibly suggest an inbuilt movement or a 'flutter' to the hard and clearly dormant patterns of nymphs I had been using. The idea of mixed hackling was an inspiration.

So I retained the basic nymphal shape of my patterns – the same shape that is in fact common to all nymphs, the humped thorax and tapered abdomen – but instead of a single coloured hackle at the head of the fly which is supposed to represent the legs I used two fine hackles – red and golden-olive – and palmered these down the full length of the abdomen, ending just above the whisks.

The change was quite remarkable.

In some light conditions the nymph appears to be nothing but a sparkle of light, with the body shape almost obscured. In others the body outline is hard and clear and the hackles are barely visible except as fine hair lines on either side. The shape of the nymph and the colour of the hackles seem to change with even the slightest movement through the light. All the time, as the nymph moved, there was this illusion of flutter, of buzz, of movement.

I had already been fishing nymphs of various patterns for some years – and with varying success – but within a few weeks the palmer dressing proved infinitely superior to all others. Not that I would make any claim to have invented such a nymph – the palmer dressing has been used by generations of fishermen. I am merely one of those anglers who have been taking part in the rediscovery of its virtues. Many others have done the same. Even while I was writing this chapter I read an article in the *Salmon and Trout Magazine* (July, 1971) by George Beal in which, dealing with dry flies, he gave the dressing of a dark olive dressed 'half palmer' – that is with the buzz of hackles reaching halfway down the shank - so that this buzz of hackles will 'give the impression of movement'.

It is the movement that attracts the fish.

X

Early Nymph Patterns—The Palmer Dressing—Methods of Tying

LAKE nymphs seem to have developed at some time before or possibly just after the period 1905–1913, but the patterns in common use at that time – and which were sometimes fished as nymphs – were the spider patterns. It was, however, common practice to use several different flies on the same cast – for example a Peter Ross as the tail fly, two or even three spiders as droppers, and a Butcher on the bob.

But it was not until 1924, with the publication of Bridgett's book on loch fishing, that something of a breakthrough occurred. By then the spiders were being dressed and designed and fished to imitate a nymph or a pupa. One of the most common patterns was the black nymph which had hackles and whisks of soft black hen or dark-speckled guinea hen, an ostrich or peacock herl body, and a fine silver wire rib.

Bridgett describes how to fish this pattern from a boat during a hatch of midge, allowing it to sink over a weed bed and bringing it up to the surface. But he would often use several different patterns on his cast during a midge hatch including the blae and black – a good imitation of the midge – and a badger hackle.

He also gives the dressings of two other nymph patterns – the olive and the green. His olive nymph had a body of swan herl dyed medium olive, ribbed with gold wire, and the hackles and whisks of olive hen. His green nymph was an apple green colour with blue hackles which he tied himself to resemble the green midge pupa and only learned later that a very similar pattern was in use on Blagdon.

But lake fishing then – as indeed it is today – was still a confusion of various styles and patterns.

By 1934, when Sidney Spencer's book on *The Art of Lake Fishing* was published, he divided lake fishing into four different styles, or groups, based upon the different patterns of 'flies' that were then in use and the different methods of fishing them.

Spencer's first group were imitations of the natural fly and the second were the nymphs. The third group were imitations or suggestions of various insects such as shrimps and beetles. The fourth group was the attractor or lure type of 'fly' – a group which included the traditional sea trout flies such as the Peter Ross, the Butcher and the Teal and Silver. He regarded these as excellent imitations of small fish or of beetles carrying bubbles of air – the silver in the dressing.

His definition of wet-fly lake fishing was 'the successful imitation of some form of underwater life upon which the trout are feeding or may be expected to feed'.

Spencer's typical nymph patterns were the March Brown, the green nymph and the black nymph, black and red spiders, and the Greenwells' Glory.

One should not, I think, attempt to make too many deductions or comparisons from these writers – or indeed from others – which relate to our own methods; nevertheless there is a clear indication from them how certain successful patterns – such as the black spider and the olive nymph – were tried and tested and handed on from one generation of lake fishermen to the next; and how, on the whole, as with the Ivens nymphs, the patterns were designed to suggest or represent a nymph rather than to copy the natural insect.

The palmer dressing had not been tried and the only attempt to suggest an inbuilt movement or 'flutter' was the use of soft hen hackles which, it was suggested, moved slightly when the nymph was pulled through the water. John Goddard has developed this idea considerably in the dressing of one of his experimental flies with very soft hair fibres.

The gill plates on the lake olive and pond olive nymphs of C. F. Walker were suggested by ostrich herl which is also soft enough to give the impression of movement. It was not until I read Kingsmill Moore that it occurred to me that the movement might be suggested even more clearly by the interplay of light among a buzz of stiff bright hackles of mixed or blended colours.

I was at that time using my own rather simplified dressing of C. F. Walker's pattern of the lake olive – which is really a golden-olive colour with a brownish thorax. So my first palmer-dressed nymphs were based on the Walker pattern but with a darker olive thorax which seemed to blend in better with the yellow seal's fur on the abdomen. I was impressed with Moore's insistence on the harmonious blending of colours. The final pattern is therefore based on the traditional palmer dressing, with the refinements of Kingsmill Moore's mixed hackles, and the general nymphal shape and colouring of C. F. Walker's lake olive. To add to its mixed parentage, however, it is only fair to point out that the original simplified lake olive dressing that I used owed a great deal to one of the river patterns of G. E. M. Skues.

The final result should not be regarded as a new pattern of fly, but rather the revival of the palmer, which is at least three or four hundred years old, adapted and refined through the work of several modern fly dressers for the special conditions of the lake.

The nymph should be tied on a down-eyed hook. In the case of large nymphs the thorax should be built up by several turns of lead wire – perhaps up to half a dozen or more – and in the case of medium sized or small nymphs the thorax can be built up by the appropriate number of turns of fine copper wire.

Having secured the wired thorax on a base of green tying silk I then tie in the two hackles at the head, just in front of the thorax. They should be fine well-balanced throat hackles with short fibres and they should be as nearly as possible the same length. I generally use a natural red cock hackle and a white cock hackle dyed a golden-olive. Furnace hackles can also be tried. On large nymphs it is sometimes necessary to add a third brown or red hackle at the head, using the other two as body hackles only.

A dab of varnish round and over the wire thorax helps to keep it secure. I then wind the silk along towards the bend where the golden pheasant topping whisks and the gold wire are tied in.

The dubbing is, in the main, seal's fur, though one can try a mixture of furs providing they are dyed the right colour. At the end of the abdomen the seal's fur should be a bright yellow – which to some extent matches and blends with the colour of the whisks – and then as one continues up the abdomen towards the thorax this should be darkened by the addition of a little olive or blue fur until by the time the thorax is reached the colour becomes a dark olive.

When the dubbing has covered the thorax allow the

tying silk to hang just behind the eye of the hook. Take the two hackles gently between the fingers and smooth the feathers together so that they are tight, side by side. Hold the tips of the hackle feathers together – either with the fingers or the hackle pliers – and take one or two turns round the head of the fly. Then, judging the distance, so that the hackling is neither too close nor too far apart, take two or three turns of hackle round the body of the nymph, finishing at the tail.

Hold the hackle points at the tail by taking two turns of the gold wire round the hook, just above the join with the whisks, and the feathers having thus been secured wind the wire up through the body of the fly, taking care not to tie down the hackles. The wire should be worked gently through the hackles with a sideways motion. The wire is tied off at the head by the silk and the end of the wire broken off. The hackle points at the tail are cut off. The fly is then completed by a whip finish behind the eye.

The dry-fly dressing is almost exactly the same except that the palmering is closer together and there is of course no bulky thorax and no lead or copper wire. For the dry fly I use the up-eyed hooks, which quite apart from the advantage in using for the dry fly is also a very good method of distinguishing it from the weighted nymphs.

This, then, is the golden-olive palmer – the nymph and the fly – and I find in practice that I use this colour, in various sizes, almost the whole season through. I used at one time to dress a black palmer and a red palmer but I must confess I have found no great advantage in doing so. Kingsmill Moore also seemed to find the golden-olive the most effective. He thought that it was based on the traditional Irish golden-olive and on the Invicta. It may be so. When it is wet the golden-olive dubbing seems to tone down very reasonably to the colour of a nymph.

What does seem to be important is to have a pleasant blend and harmony of colouring – and having written those words they remind me that they are almost precisely the same words as those used more than a century ago by men like Cutcliffe and Pulman – who were two of the greatest fly dressers of their time or indeed of any time. Pulman, I remember, emphasized very strongly the need to create 'a harmony of colours' between the hackle and the dubbing. Mixed hackling helps to create this harmony.

These 19th century palmer patterns were mostly for dry fly work on fast streams and they must have floated well. Pulman's red palmer had a peacock herl body, ribbed with gold twist, and a cock's hackle wound thickly round the head but sparsely round the body. His blue palmer was based on the two West Country patterns of the blue dun and the blue upright. The whisks were fibres from a blue cock's hackle, the body of mole fur ribbed with gold silk, and the body and head hackle of blue hen. But he would mix the colours of his dubbing and during the mayfly season the overall colour of the fly was much nearer to a golden-olive than a blue dun.

George Beal's half-palmers are really what the name indicates – they are hackled from the eye of the hook to the middle of the shank. For the large dark olive he uses two hackles wound on together – one of a dark rusty black and the other a grey. The hook is size 12 or 13 and the silk dark olive.

All these patterns – indeed the whole principle of the palmer dressing – create merely an illusion of the natural insect. In doing so, of course, size is of great importance. On some small lochans I have used palmers on size 15 and 16 hooks, with success, while palmers on 12 or 13 have been ignored. I have almost come to the tentative conclusion that size may well be more important than colour.

But that is another heresy!

XI

Dry Flies and Open Water—Watching for the Hatch—The Immortal Passion

GOD forbid! – I would not have you believe all your troubles are over if you fish a palmer-dressed nymph, that this is some magic that will make you into a good fisherman overnight, for it will not. It will do you no more good than any other pattern if you fish it clumsily and without imagination, without the infinite subtleties of presentation that are needed.

I would not have angling overlaid with science, says Howard Marshall, and quite right too, because there is a certain magic in our craft which seems to be inherent in the primitive instinct of man, which has in it some of the inherited logic of the wilderness, the ancient skills of our ancestors. Nor would I have it overlaid with complexity either. We have for too long been bedevilled on our lakes with a frantic confusion of conflicting voices.

It was a relief to discover there is no need to listen too closely to such voices, that one can fish one pattern of nymph and one pattern of fly throughout the year . . . all the year long, 'morning and evening, windie or cloudie' . . . and in so doing concentrate on the art of its presentation to the fish to the exclusion of all other less important matters.

This is by no means something that happens only on the lake.

Howard Marshall has pointed out that though it may be heresy to say so there is many a good chalk stream angler – such as Richard Threlfall with his palmer-dressed fly – who fishes only one pattern of dry fly year in and year out and 'does as well as many men and a good deal better than most'. It may well be that some of us will get great enjoyment from using an infinite variety of patterns of nymphs but as Sawyer has shown us we can get great execution from using one. Indeed I have a feeling that to fish one pattern truly well is as much as most of us can manage in a lifetime.

One has to build up and acquire a sense of what I can only describe as watercraft. One has to learn to appreciate certain things by instinct – which is perhaps another word for acquired experience – and to develop certain subtleties of behaviour, certain perceptions of the mind, and of the imagination.

One should not, for example, ever disregard the opportunity of fishing a surface fly.

Hugh Sheringham, one time angling editor of *The Field*, who mostly fished Blagdon with the wet fly – and very large ones at that – nevertheless admitted in a delightful article published in 1913 that he had known nothing more exciting and fascinating 'on that wonderful lake' than the two or three good evening rises there which had given him 'a fair chance to fish dry'.

For the sheer pleasure and excitement of it – do not disregard such a chance.

It does not, I think, come very often, and that is why I mostly fish the nymph. The rise of olives or sedges at Weir Wood or Blagdon or Two Lakes is fairly limited and scattered and one has to wait for the opportunity. But when it comes – how exciting it can be!

So I will now tell you a little story of what happened to me some years ago at Weir Wood.

I was seated on the shore near one of the shallow bays on the south bank where the weed growth is thick and the rushes are high along the edge, leaving open patches of water. As I was eating my sandwiches I saw some grousewing hatching quite close inshore. So – just in case – I put on a sedge pattern of about the right size and colour. In those days I palmer-hackled my sedges, of course, but I also dressed them with wings as well. They look nice with wings.

But nothing happened and no trout moved so I went on eating.

Along came one of the rods, a cheerful fellow who had also been having lunch on the bank somewhere further up. He had a boat beached near and was on his way back. He asked me what fly I was using and I showed him. He himself had been using a black lure.

So we sit and talk for a minute or so and I point to one of the grousewings that had settled on the rushes. He seemed to be rather surprised.

'Do you always match the fly on the water?'

No, I say, not always.

Then it happens.

One always expects it to happen and yet one always seems to be taken by surprise when it does. There was a rise in the shallows – quite close in – barely a yard from the mud and pebbles on the edge. The trout must have come in very close indeed and I daresay would not have done so had we not been sitting down, well hidden, about ten yards from the side.

So I kneel down and cast from where I am – and the first time my fly lands on the mud about a foot short of the water. Fortunately it does not stick and comes away and the second time the fly falls about three or four feet out in the shallows – with most of the nylon cast and all of the line lying on the bank. Those trout were very close in – I daresay in not much more than a foot of water. Fortunately the fly fell delicately and did not scare them – a nymph might – and it was well taken after floating there for not more than a few seconds.

Something told me – instinct or experience, I haven't the least idea – not to go near the water. I stayed where I was and dragged that trout up on to the mud and sideways through the shallows to the rushes so that when I could grab him and pick him up he was several yards away from the area of the rise. Fortunately he was not a large fish – just under three-quarters of a pound.

But I had done the correct thing – I had not disturbed the water – and when I had unhooked the trout and looked to see what was happening the rise was still going on. There were other trout there and they were still feeding on the grousewing.

Of course, it was very exciting – and my companion gave a great cheer and a whoop and was away to his boat which was beached about forty yards off along the bank. It was precisely the wrong thing to do, and I knew it, but it was too late to do or say anything to stop him. I had caught a trout in my way and he was going to catch one in his.

But not these trout.

The boat came along in a great flurry of ripples and he was standing up in it – yes, actually standing up – casting a long line and a heavy black lure on the end of it. Splosh! Bang! He didn't get within twenty yards before the rise stopped and the trout fled. They must have been scared out of their lives. They were close to the surface, in very shallow water, and they could see the arrival of this creature on their horizon very clearly – quite apart from the sound of the ripples splashing on the boat and the sound of the fly splashing into the water. Oh, dear me, it was very sad and very tragic and I never got another rise like that all day, but what I think is perhaps even more sad is that my companion of the black lure had simply no idea at all what he had done wrong and why the rise stopped just as he was getting into the right position to cover it.

That is what I mean by the need to develop a sense of watercraft – the knowledge of how fish will react and what they will do and how and when they eat and how they will be scared – and how not to scare them.

During a hatch of olives I do not use an exact imitation – merely an unweighted golden-olive palmer-dressed fly on a size 12 or 14 hook. For a hatch of sedge I use a red palmer on a 10 or 12 hook – sometimes scuttering it across the surface. Strangely enough I have never bothered to tie a special dressing for fishing the midge and during a midge hatch I will as often as not use either a floating palmer or an ordinary palmer-nymph fished just below the surface. I persistently fish a nymph even during a hatch of caenis. I seem to do no worse than those who attempt to imitate these tiny little flies.

There are still one or two special patterns of dry flies that I carry though I can hardly remember when they were last used. I have a nice imitation of the crane fly – the daddy longlegs – which once did great execution at Weir Wood one hot August day some eight or ten years ago. I also carry a nice pattern of the red ant and one of the black – though I do not recollect using either.

But – there – I have not the 'immortal passion' for the dry fly about which David Jacques writes so lovingly and fluently. Not that we conflict too greatly. My own best passion is for a nymph gliding just below the surface so that in fact there is but a few bare inches between us. To me, one of the great advantages of the nymph is that it can be animated, can be made to move, and in the creation of the movement there is a continual fascination and challenge. A dry fly is – mostly – static. It floats and is watched.

On the other hand John Henderson, who is a devoted dry fly man on lakes and reservoirs, has developed techniques which are far from static. One of them is floating the dry fly with the wind, and keeping pace with it by walking along the bank.

There are techniques in both nymph and dry-fly fishing which we are only beginning to explore. One of them is – simply – the creation of a hatch. For this it is necessary to discover a good bed of weed not too far under the surface and within reasonable casting distance of the shore. The angler must be well hidden. He casts his nymph persistently to precisely the same place over the weed, allowing it to sink as close to the surface of the weed as possible, then giving an induced take so that the nymph comes quickly to the surface, and then gliding it gradually back until he can lift and cast again to the same spot. He never alters the length of line he has out and he always casts to the same place.

The theory is simple. Cruising trout have sharp eyes and they are always on the look-out for food. If they see what appear to be nymphs rising regularly in one place they may well cruise over to that place to investigate. It is an adaptation of George La Branche's technique for the dry fly on rivers – casting continually to one place to give the impression of a hatch. Whether it will work on the lake I do not know. It is true that I have taken trout by this method of continually casting in one place but whether I actually attracted the trout to come there or whether there were trout there already before I started I am not able to say. But by the use of one's imagination and a modicum of inventiveness even on a dull day fishing can be interesting.

I suppose that nine out of ten of my fish are taken on the nymph but some of the most exciting fishing I have ever had was to the dry fly. It has a superb and exciting quality which is purely its own. It is unwise to underrate the capacity of the trout to take the surface fly. Lure men will tell you that dry-fly fishing is worthless. So it is – for them. They have not the watercraft to make it worthwhile. It is something that is outside their experience.

During a hatch of olives it is often valuable to change over for a short time to a surface fly. This can be floated in the area of the hatch and sometimes even pulled very gently along. One should, wherever possible, cast to the rise and let it float there for some time. It is enormously exciting and rewarding when your fly is suddenly engulfed, without warning, by a large trout.

Trout can be made to rise to the dry fly – of that there is no doubt. I remember once bringing my fly very slowly in towards the bank in preparation for a lift off and a new cast. It was no more than three or four yards out and drifting very slowly in over the calm surface. There was no sign of a fish anywhere. Suddenly a dark shape seemed to disengage itself from the weeds almost directly under the fly and I was suddenly aware of a large brown trout rising slowly to the surface. One could feel – yes feel – the sudden intensity of that fish as it moved up for the kill. I was more or less paralysed with astonishment. There was my fly drifting in and there was this huge fish rising up very very slowly to intercept it. It was a very small fly and it was a very large fish. Who says that a big trout will not move very far to take a tiny insect? This one moved upwards every bit of five or six feet and he took that fly on the surface with one large snap of his jaws. I do not think I actually tightened into that fish. I merely shook with excitement and the hook went home. He came out at something just over four pounds.

Then there was the monster at Two Lakes who actually jumped out of the water – or so it seemed to me – to take my fly just as it landed. He was a devil of a big fish and he turned and took me right into the weeds and snapped the *6* lb nylon at the knot as easily as cotton. I still feel a sense of awe when I think of that fish.

On both these occasions there was a hatch of olives – a limited hatch, not very widespread, just a few flies here and there taking off from the water. An unweighted golden-olive palmer greased to float was the fly that both these fish took. It may be my imagination but I have never yet taken a poor fish on a dry fly – they have all seemed to be at least average or else well above average size. Some people will tell you that it is only the biggest trout that have the taste for the surface insect, and one of the best anglers that I know at Two Lakes fishes very little else.

XII

Lines and Spaces

WILSON Stephens, editor of *The Field*, once encouraged me to write an article on the philosophy of fly-fishing. It was an attempt to find out the common springs that all men share who suffer from the passion of the fly.

There are many by-products of fishing and one is certainly the friendships and companionships that one picks up on the way, often casually enough, and often to find with some surprise how insidiously they have enriched your life; and to fly-fish is also a therapy that will mend some of the tatters of our working lives and sieve out much of the dregs of anxiety from our brains – but we do not go fishing entirely for these things however important they become.

There is some other driving force that pushes us irresistibly towards the river or the lake, almost as if we were returning home, to a wife or mistress, for some deep comfort that we can rarely describe because it is also an intense excitement – some esoteric passion of body and mind which seems to have within it the illogicality of a faith. It is in some ways to reduce its stature to describe it as a hobby or a sport.

Partly – or even considerably – it is also the urge within us to escape from the intensive pressure of our lives and from our surroundings. It is not entirely coincidence that the most passionate fishermen seem to be those who live in the vast industrial cities and conurbations. Most of us suffer from megapolis. The vast built-up areas – the pressure of nine million neighbours – may as yet be too great for our unadaptable natures especially if we are still peasants at heart. We are said to be gregarious but the truth may be that we cannot stand to be overcrowded for too long at a time however much we like our fellow men, and that there is no need to adopt Rousseau's concept of the noble savage to explain our feeling that there is often something inhuman in an over-concentration of humanity.

This thread of thinking – this desire for escape – is very noticeable in the writing of many who have been dedicated fly fishers. It is there in all of us; and certainly those who have not lived in London are unlikely to understand the passion of citizens who want to escape from it. Their longing for the joys which are not to be found in cities – the words are those of Edward Grey – seems to expand in direct proportion to the intolerable burden of their captivity.

Grey was a politician – and John Waller Hills was another – who wrote with considerable feeling of the wild delirium of excitement that possessed them when they could escape from the House of Commons to take the late night or early morning train to Stockbridge or to Inverness.

There was always this sense of 'escape'.

But we would not necessarily have this same feeling at all if we were about to take a job as a deckhand on a trawler or a netsman in an estuary, so we cannot put it down entirely to the catching of fish. Why, then, do we feel this delirious happiness at the thought of fly fishing?

I do not know whether I have the answer; but I think

I have part of it, or enough to point us on the way, and though it is true that when we go fishing we 'shake hands with the caveman' – as Howard Marshall puts it – there is also more in it than a return to the savage pre-occupations of our ancesters.

And a great part of the answer was put in a book by H. B. McCaskie which was published some twenty years ago. I do not know Mr McCaskie or indeed anything about him – though he may well be the creator of the fly known as McCaskie's Green Cat and if so was therefore one of the great fishing companions of G. E. M. Skues – but he has the heart of the matter close to his pen. Fishing, at one time, he says, was merely a means of obtaining food and filling an unoccupied hour, but when the industrial revolution herded the population into the towns then to go fishing became a symbol of something more than an escape. It was a return to the freedom and beauty of the old life, a return to a cleaner and saner and more human form of existence. Escape – says McCaskie – is not the right word. The Greeks had a better. They called it ecstasy – which meant a withdrawal, a standing aside.

Ecstasy is almost the same as the 'immortal passion' of Jacques and this same theme recurs again and again in the works of writers from Kingsley to Dunne, to Grey and Marshall and Plunket Greene – the list is endless. They do not necessarily use the word ecstasy but when Grey tells of the unspeakable joy of being swept clean of all consciousness of self when he is tramping the Scottish moors and when Marshall feels himself integrated with the springs and origins of human existence as he watches the life of the River Lambourn they are conveying the essence of what it means.

It is a humbling thought that it is not alone 'the atavistic pleasures of the chase' which take us to the water, that it is not solely 'an escape from the market place', not entirely the delight of holding a weapon in our hands, even if it is only a weapon of split cane, but that all these are part of a greater fulfilment, which is spiritual.

Perhaps we are putting it too high, or in too high-flown language, and I would not like to be thought of as too much of an aesthete any more than I would like to be considered a mystic; nevertheless, if mountaineers can commune with God upon the high peaks of the Karakoram I do not see why a nymph fisherman could not at least be allowed a little pantheism by the lake. If it is there that we feel close to the springs and origins of our existence then we ought to be permitted to say so. It is right to touch on the theme even if we are not competent to elaborate. It does explain a part of our happiness.

A moment ago I used the word 'aesthete' and I think it is true that fly fishing contains within its nature a considerable aesthetic pleasure – a pleasure which in many cases can be intensely intellectual as well as atavistic and is compounded with the physical exhilaration of rhythms and skills which are difficult to acquire and profoundly satisfying to employ – such as the considerable delight in the power thrust of a double-handed salmon fly-rod sending the line straight and true to its destination.

Which brings us back to the truism that there is more to fishing than catching fish. So there is – yet it would be no good if we didn't catch them. It is why we are there. But the point I would make – and it is the point that is implicit in most of the earlier chapters – is that the greatest pleasure and satisfaction in fishing can only come to us if we use the most delicate and skilful and – yes, let us use the word – the most artistic method of doing so. We have a delicate craft. It has been handed down to us for our own particular delight and it is worth the conservation.

And as for the other pleasures that come of their own accord in the beauty of our surroundings they have never been put better than by Edward Grey:

> . . . the pure act of breathing at such times seems glorious. People talk of being a child of nature, and moments such as these are the times when it is possible to feel so; to know the full joy of animal life – to desire nothing beyond. There are times when I have stood still for joy of it all, on my way through the freedom of a Highland moor, and felt the wind and looked upon the mountains and the sky, till I felt conscious only of the strength of a mighty current of life which swept away all consciousness of self and made me a part of all I beheld.

There is not one of us who has not felt something of the kind. Pantheism or mysticism – call it what you will – the experience is too strong to be dubbed an illusion or an escape. It is more desirable than either. As Howard Marshall puts it:

> . . . one becomes involved in the life cycle of insect and fish, is at one with the organic growth of everything in the valley. From the caddis to the sedge, from the darting nymph to the emerging mayfly, everything is part of a living pattern in which the angler participates.

Or to put it in another way, there is the story of the elderly and distinguished member of my club who was asked what he thought were the greatest things he had achieved in life. He was indeed a very distinguished old gentleman with a string of letters after his name and a public reputation. He thought it over for a while and then he said there were only two things he had experienced in his life which had completely satisfied him, physically and emotionally and intellectually, and to which he felt he had been able to devote his entire abilities and talents, and by which he had felt completely fulfilled and absorbed, and one of these was going fishing and the other was making love.

Bibliography

Bridgett, R. C., *Loch Fishing in Theory and Practice*, Jenkins, 1924.

Dunne, J. W., *Sunshine and the Dry Fly*, Black, 1924.

Frost, W. E., and Brown, M. E., *The Trout*, Collins, 1967.

Goddard, John, *Trout Flies of Still-Water*, Black, 1970.

Grey of Fallodon, Earl, *Fly Fishing*, Dent, 1907.

Harris, J. R., *An Angler's Entomology*, Collins, 1952.

Henzell, H. P., *The Art and Craft of Loch Fishing*, Allan, 1937.

Hills, John Waller, *A History of Fly Fishing for Trout*, Allan, 1921.

Ivens, T. C., *Still Water Fly Fishing*, Deutsch, 1st Edn., 1953, 3rd Edn., 1971.

Jacques, David, *Fisherman's Fly*, Black, 1965.

Kite, Oliver, *Nymph Fishing in Practice*, Jenkins, 1963, and *A Fisherman's Diary*, Deutsch, 1969.

Lane, Joscelyn, *Lake and Loch Fishing*, Seeley Service, 1954.

Lawrie, W. H., *A Reference Book of English Trout Flies*, Pelham Books, 1967.

Marshall, Howard, *Reflections on a River*, Witherby, 1967.

McCaskie, H. B., *The Guileless Trout*, Cresset Press, 1950.

Moore, T. C. Kingsmill, *A Man May Fish*, Jenkins, 1960.

Oatts, H. A., *Loch Trout*, Jenkins, 1958.

Plunket Greene, Harry, *Where the Bright Waters Meet*, 2nd Edn., Witherby, 1969.

Phillips, Ernest, *Trout in Lakes and Reservoirs*, Longmans, 1914.

Sawyer, Frank, *Nymph and the Trout*, Black, 2nd Edn., 1971.

Skues, G. E. M., *The Way of a Trout with a Fly*, Black, 4th Edn., 1949.

Spencer, Sidney, *The Art of Lake Fishing*, Witherby, 1934.

Veniard, John, *Reservoir and Lake Flies*, Black, 1970, which includes the article by John Henderson on lake fishing.

Walker, C. F., *Lake Flies and their Imitation*, Jenkins, 1960.

Williams, A. Courtney, *A Dictionary of Trout Flies*, Black, 4th Edn., 1965, 5th Edn., 1972.

Index